Worshiping in the
Small Membership Church

WORSHIPING IN THE SMALL MEMBERSHIP CHURCH

Copyright © 2008 by Abingdon Press

All rights reserved.

This book is printed on acid-free paper.

Library of Congress Cataloging-in-Publication Data

Wallace, Robin Knowles.
    Worshiping in the small membership church/ Robin Knowles Wallace.
        p. cm.—(Ministry in the small membership church)
    Includes bibliographical references.
    ISBN 978-0-687-65101-6 (pbk. : alk. paper)
    1. Public worship.   2. Small churches.   I. Title.

    BV15.W335 2008
    264—dc22

2007040810

All scripture quotations are from the New Revised Standard Version of the Bible, copyright 1989, Division of Christian Education of the National Council of the Churches of Christ in the United States of America. Used by permission. All rights reserved.

08 09 10 11 12 13 14 15 16 17—10 9 8 7 6 5 4 3 2 1

MANUFACTURED IN THE UNITED STATES OF AMERICA

To the congregations and groups with whom I have worshiped,
where size did not matter

Thanks

To family, friends, and colleagues in ministry who read the draft: John Wallace, Millard Knowles, Laura Wallace, Joanmarie Smith, Mark Parsons, Margie MacAskie, and Cindy Glocke. To the Trustees of Methodist Theological School in Ohio and Dean John Kampen for granting me a Faculty Fellowship for sabbatical so that, among other things, I could write this book uninterrupted. To students at MTSO and the Course of Study School of Ohio for helping me think about these ideas and their application. To Grace Wallace, who listened to it all. Finally, to Sarah Lancaster and Lisa Withrow, wonderful colleagues who encourage, challenge, and make lunchtimes such a delight.

117814

Begin Where You Are: Involving the Congregation in Worship Leadership and Participation

In the beginning... God saw that it was good. (Genesis 1)

To the Pastor

You have been called to empower and "to equip the saints for the work of ministry, for building up the body of Christ" (Ephesians 4:12). God has given you gifts for this work, and the church has most likely provided you with training for it. You are blessed to have answered that call, and more blessings await. At this point you are working with a worshiping congregation of up to one hundred persons. Be content where you are (Philippians 4:11); get to know your congregation; love them through the Spirit; find what gifts God has given them. Sometimes as pastors we may think that we have to do everything: pick the hymns and scriptures, prepare the sermon and bulletins, set out the paraments and offering plates, greet people, give them bulletins, play the piano, lead the singing, pray all prayers, preach, collect the offering, and so on. This isn't what our call is—our call is to equip others for this work of ministry so that the body of Christ might be built up in this place. Involving persons in liturgy, that is, "the work of the people on behalf of the world," is holy work. Pray that you may thrive and struggle with involving people so that God's church might be built up.

To the Worship Leader

You have been called out of the congregation to assist in the leadership of worship in your congregation. God and your congregation or pastor have noted those gifts in you. This book is meant to travel with you on this journey, along with your own preparation, prayer, and other resources (books, classes, persons, websites) you will find on the way. This is holy work to which you are called. Use it to grow in your own faith and in holiness so that you may point to Jesus Christ without getting in the way. Like the pastor, "equip the saints for the work of ministry, for building up the body of Christ" (Ephesians 4:12). Pray that all you do may build up and equip others through love and patience.

To the Congregation

You have been called to speak "the truth in love" and "grow up in every way into him who is the head, into Christ" (Ephesians 4:15). You are no mere bystander to the work that is worship—you are needed in preparation and prayer, in participation and listening, in singing and responding. God has placed gifts in you that can be used for worship. These gifts may be obvious or they may not. With your pastor and worship leader, be willing to uncover your gifts and strengthen them for the glory of God.

Take your faith and your worship seriously and joyfully that they may be for you the blessing God intends. Pray that you may do your part that the worship of God may be full.

Discerning Our Gifts

A simple walk through an ordinary worship service suggests some of the gifts that are needed or useful in worship. Not all of them are required for "good" worship, but any or all of them might enhance our worship and deepen our worship experience. The varieties of gifts mentioned remind us that it is good that people have different gifts (1 Corinthians 12:4-11). David Ray commented in *Small Churches Are the Right Size*, that out of fifty persons in worship on a Sunday, forty-five could very easily have been involved in some leadership, helping worship happen.[1] Lyle Schaller suggests that even three to seven volunteers in a small congregation can make a big difference.[2] And in a house church or emerging church, some of the tasks will be assigned very organically, by whose home is the meeting place, and so on.

In some congregations there may be a cluster of gifts around a particular area—a culture or art form, a mission or program; is this your church's niche and can you evangelize around those gifts? Other congregations might be missing something that is listed below; does it matter to your congregation or is that not where the Spirit is calling you at the present time? You can "get by" as a worshiping group without some of the gifts on this list, except for radical hospitality—it is vital!

Discerning gifts can be done as an interest survey, either written or done verbally in small groups or one-on-one (see appendix 1). Include all ages (from about four years old on up) and all members of the congregation, including those who may not be able to attend services. This work will be more effective if you combine it with two things: (1) Don't just ask people if they want to be an usher or play an instrument. Consider the gifts needed for the tasks because the discerning activity sometimes brings a realization that we do have the right gifts for a task and just didn't realize it. Then, offer training for persons for different tasks and make it happen. (See "Equipping the Saints," p. 17.) (2) Ask people to list the gifts they see in others. It has become a tradition in some preschools and elementary schools to sit in a circle on someone's birthday and go around, having each person share something good about the birthday child. Could we do this as a worshiping community or in a small group, thinking about the varieties of gifts used in worshiping God? What if a congregation had a "thanksgiving" service for the gifts God had placed among them and worked hard at naming those gifts in each other? There needs to be safe and prayerful space for this discussion, but it could yield very important results for people's lives as well as for the worship in your community.

Here's a description of some of the gifts God has given to help us worship together (see appendix 1 for complete listing):

❑ Someone who can produce and place signs with directions to the church and worship times. This includes physical signs on roadsides and near your meeting place, as well as voicemail messages, notices in the local news media, and on a church website. Parking spots marked for visitors is also a generous gesture. Gifts needed: construction, artwork, publicity, and communication.

❑ People who are radically hospitable, looking for the Christ in each visitor or stranger, to greet at the doorways and to be watchful for latecomers in the service, ready to greet them during any informal times in worship and after the service.[3] The traditional use of ushers fits in this grouping, as ushers often pass out bulletins or have other tasks of helping persons settle in for worship, finding seats, discovering where the nursery is, taking the offering, helping during the service if persons need hymnals or Bibles or the microphones reset. Gifts needed: computer or typing skills to prepare "friendship folders," willingness to stop a chat with a longtime friend to speak to someone new, having courage to talk with strangers, looking for those who might be left out, sensitivity to visitors' comfort levels in wanting to be involved, skills of oversight and detail management. One note about the gift of radical hospitality: if it is not present in some form in your congregation, there will be no space for Jesus Christ, so work on this one because it is essential!

❑ Persons to prepare the space for worship. This includes unlocking the doors, cleaning the worship space, making certain that resources like Bibles and hymnals are available as needed (or projection and slides are ready), preparing bulletins or worship guides, putting out paraments, gathering any visual art for the worship theme, getting the wicks on the candles free for lighting, having matches or a lighter available, gathering flowers for the altar or caring for plants in the worship space, making offering plates available, moving chairs around if necessary, marking the Bible that will be read from, turning the heat up or the fans on or opening windows, shoveling snow or raking leaves from the front sidewalk, getting sound equipment ready, ringing the church bell, preparing the baptismal water for pouring into the font, preparing the communion bread and juice or wine and the vessels needed. In the tradition of the church, many of these tasks belonged to the sacristan. In the service itself, lighting candles, bringing offering plates from the altar to the ushers, and assisting with communion are often tasks of one or two acolytes, from children who have been trained for these tasks up to adults. Gifts needed: housekeeping, artistic, attention to detail, bread baking, sewing, gardening, some muscle; note that many of these gifts are small and can be done by faithful persons of any age.

❑ Persons to lead congregational singing or accompany it. Many churches need to think a little outside of the box for these gifts. Keyboard (piano, organ, and synthesizer) skills are useful, but so are violin, flute, guitar, string bass or cello, dulcimer (hammered or plucked), recorder, or saxophone. Average singing voices with sufficient courage and thoughtful preparation can lead singing. Simple percussion instruments or small bells might also be used to enhance worship, during a processional or at appropriate moments in baptism or communion. There may be persons who are not strong singers but who have a good sense for picking the appropriate song for the appropriate moment. Gifts needed: playing any musical instrument, contributions toward buying or renting instruments or paying for music lessons, courage, a steady sense of rhythm, the ability to discern the right music at the right time, the willingness to be vulnerable and flexible, and the willingness to encourage others' musical gifts.

❏ Persons to read scripture in worship. If there is a tradition of giving Bibles to children at a certain age, work with them to read in worship in the following months. If you have persons who speak languages other than your native tongue, involve them in reading scripture on Pentecost and at other times of the year to remind the congregation of God's love for the whole world. Memorizing the most important verse or phrase of the scripture allows it to be delivered "by heart" with strong eye contact with the congregation. Gifts needed: clear voice, good eye contact, appropriate sense of dramatic reading, willingness to research a bit of the background of the reading,[4] willingness to rehearse with others when the scripture contains several characters; broad age range is very appropriate here.

❏ Persons to lead other parts of the service. This might include leading responsive Psalm readings or calls to worship, praying a set prayer over the offering, calling for announcements, reading prayer request cards, reading a contemporary passage that complements the scripture. Whereas scriptures are most often read up front while standing, you might consider having other parts of the service read by someone who must remain seated. Gifts needed: clear voice, engaging presence, broad age range.

❏ Persons to lead prayers and persons to pray one-on-one with others. It is very important for pastors and worship leaders to discover who are the "prayer warriors" in the congregation. These persons have a passion for prayer, a belief in its power, and the willingness to pray constantly. Some of them may also be willing to share these skills in worship leadership, gathering the prayer joys and concerns of the congregation and weaving them into a congregational prayer. Others may be more comfortable praying with persons one-on-one at special opportunities for prayer, at the end of the service or communion or during a prayer and healing service. There may also be persons who don't see themselves having gifts of prayer but who might be interested in studying and working on those gifts and then sharing. Gifts needed: a prayer life, passion for and belief in the power of prayer, willingness to hear others' joys and concerns and hold them together before God.

❑ Persons to work on involving toddlers, children, and youth in worship. This may include leading times with children (often called "children's moments" or "story for all ages"). It is important for the pastor to lead these times enough so that the children know that she or he is their pastor, too. But it is also something for which others may well have gifts. In addition, toddlers and younger children may be able to help prepare or clean up the worship space, grow flowers for the altar, contribute artwork. Older children and youth can effectively participate in a variety of worship leadership positions—have an adult keep an eye out for their talents and gently show them how those talents and their interests have a place in worship. Gifts needed: respect for children and youth, knowledge of their developmental stages including faith development, storytelling gifts, interest in what children have to say, willingness to pass on the faith and its traditions, flexibility for when children "go off track" to go there if the Spirit leads or gently lead things back, and patience.

❑ Persons to pick out, adapt, or write worship materials, prayers, scripture dramas. If you have persons who are interested in theatre/drama, having them read the upcoming scriptures and set them as minidramas when appropriate is a simple way to add interest to worship. Gifts needed: a love of planning and reading scripture and prayer books, a sense of what is appropriate in worship with your particular congregation, love of words and skill with them, possibility thinkers.

❑ Persons to enrich worship through other media. These might include painting, sculpture, metalwork, making candles, preparing PowerPoint presentations, making a short video, finding a film clip or piece of music for a theme or to illustrate a sermon point, or woodworking. Gifts needed: interest in or skills in any of the arts and an understanding of how God uses art in worship to "speak" to us.[5]

❑ Persons to work on larger celebrations, such as homecoming or a special music, arts, or seasonal Sunday or service. Gifts needed: a love of planning and organization, follow-through, creativity, love of people, team players (these events are not one-person shows), as well as a knowledge of talents and services available in the area.

❑ Persons to serve communion. Two of the "rediscoveries" of the liturgical renewal over the last twenty-five years have been that (1) an important aspect of communion is receiving it as gift and (2) serving communion, sharing the gift of it with a congregation, is a blessing. So, more and more churches are training laypersons to serve communion. Gifts needed: graciousness, eye contact, hospitality, and a strong back if persons are kneeling at a communion rail.

❑ Persons to support others in baptismal vows. Many churches include sponsors for baptized persons, part of the tradition of the church, to support them in prayer and follow up after their baptism. These persons also stand with the person during the actual baptism, no matter what their age. Gifts needed: supportive personality, willingness to share one's faith and encourage others in their faith journey, mature faith, openness to journeys that are different than one's own, good listening skills.

❑ Persons to discuss the upcoming sermon with the pastor in Bible study. In order to prepare sermons that are a real meeting point between scripture and the congregation, many churches have a group of persons who study the Scriptures together and "feed forward"[6] (instead of "feeding back") to the sermon; the group needs to be clear about what things are confidential and what might be shared with the congregation. Gifts needed: love of scripture, openness and willingness to study it and struggle with it in the light of issues of the day and of the congregation.

❑ Persons to study a theological issue to share with the congregation in building up/growing faithfulness. Sometimes communities and congregations have issues that would benefit from theological study. One issue in my state currently is the reopening of coal mines, which raises a number of questions for Christians: What does Scripture and the church say about our use of the earth? What do they say about economics and the need for persons for jobs to feed and clothe their families? What responsibilities do Christians have as employers, employees, business owners,

owners of land, campers, farmers, parents, and grandparents? A group of persons who are willing to research and reflect on these issues and then find a way to present them before God in worship can help all of us grapple with our own faithfulness. Gifts needed: energy around an issue, an open mind, research and analysis skills, maturity to hold opposing views in tension and grapple with God's will.

Equipping the Saints

Once you have conducted the surveys (appendix 1) with as many persons as possible, gather a group to sift through what you have learned.

Most important, do you have the essential gifts for radical hospitality? If so, then move on to the next paragraph. If not, take some time to pray, study, and worship together around the radical nature of Jesus' hospitality and how he taught and modeled it for us (stated most clearly in Matthew 25:31-46). This is a welcoming and sharing that respects diversity, difference, and boundaries; it calls forth that same respect from everyone we meet. You don't need to be a certain age to be radically hospitable—sometimes children are the most welcoming among us. You don't have to be an extrovert or "hugger," but you do need to make space that is safe and welcoming for others who come to worship with you. Radical hospitality is important to practice in worship and with each other so that doing it at home, at work, at school, in the community, will become more and more natural and habitual for us. This is the love Jesus called us to, not sentimental or soft, but strong, nurturing, respectful, mature, serving, not because we have to, but because we know that we have been loved so fully in that way by God that we want to share it with the world.

Next, look at where clusters of gifts are—around the arts, around planning and organization, around scripture or prayer. Are you surprised about this clustering? If not, then just some tweaking may be needed to include more persons and more of that gift in your worship times. If so, then strategize by discussing the following questions:

1. How well formed are these interests and skills in these persons? Is this gift a fit with at least part of our congregation? (See also #4 below.)
2. If there are several persons with interests or skills, could we gather them as a group to share their skills and interests with one another?
3. What sort of training would these persons need in order to use these gifts in worship?
    a. Beginning where we are, does the pastor or worship leader have skills and understanding about the use of these gifts in worship?
    b. How much do these persons need to learn about the language of worship? Part of learning a sport is not simply how to run and throw, but understanding the language of the game—What is a base? A three-point basket? What does second and goal mean? Similarly, worship has a language that assists us in learning to participate in it more fully. Studying the Glossary in this book is a good place to start, as are explanations in Children's Moments, newsletter articles, and classes.
    c. Is there a person who uses this gift in worship at another church or through a seminary who might come talk with us or lead a workshop?
    d. Are there workshops or classes through seminaries or church organizations that we might send these persons to in order to increase their understanding of how to use these gifts in worship?
    e. Are there books or videos that demonstrate the use of these gifts in worship?
4. Will there be any hesitation or impediment to the use of this gift in worship?
    a. Is this gift appropriate for our worship? Why? (The ability to theologically articulate this will be important for its acceptance. Many people will open

themselves to new things if they understand that it is theologically appropriate for worship.)

   b. How can we educate the congregation on the value of this gift for our worship?

   c. Reduce anxieties around the use of this gift in worship by saying something like "We think this gift could enrich our worship and help us worship God in some new and spiritual ways. We would like to try it for this service/six weeks/at this time so that our sisters and brothers might have a voice in our worship together. For the love of God and each other, let's open ourselves to do this together."

5. How do we make room in our worship for these gifts to be shared?

   a. Do we want to have a special service highlighting these gifts?

   b. Are these gifts organic to us as a congregation, and should they be used every week?

   c. Is there a seasonal way to add this element, for example, art during Advent, a new kind of praying during Lent, communion during the summer months where the Scriptures focus on Jesus as the Bread of Life?

Next, are you seeing gifts that are already in use? How well are they being used? Has someone been doing a particular task for so long that they are burned out on it, even though they have the skills? Could they train someone to assist with that task or to trade off with them? Finding new or younger persons who have interests or gifts that are already present provides good avenues for passing on traditions and values that the community deems important in their worship practices. Those who do the training can pass on traditions without binding new persons to "there's only one way." Teaching someone new how to do a task is a good time to revisit why we do it in this way as well as what the other options are. That revisiting and training can also give renewed energy for the task or simply relief that there is someone else capable of assisting. Pastors, it is your task to equip, sometimes for worship will ensure that they are conducive to the worship experience of the whole.

As you prepare to have various gifts shared in worship, remember the words of 1 Corinthians 12:12-26: We are one body in Christ with many members, all of which are important to the whole. So don't let any one person's gift dominate and make certain that each has a part or voice as she or he desires and is appropriate in worship.

Periodically look at what you as pastor or worship leader are doing. Is there something that the congregation or trained persons in the congregation could do? Here are several simple changes that might happen as a result of discerning, equipping, and using the worship gifts of the congregation:

❑ A Call to Worship based on the scripture is written by a middle-school student and engages the congregation through participation and sets the theme for worship as the first thing. Not only are the student's parents proud, but former Sunday school teachers and the confirmation leader take joy in how she has grown in faith.

❑ A congregation that is lucky enough to have a choir joins them on a prayer response that the choir has sung for a month this summer. For some persons, this adds a blessing to the prayer time together.

❑ A third-grade acolyte steps gracefully to the altar and takes the collection plates to an usher. Not only is his own sense of belonging in worship enhanced, but it keeps him in worship and leaves the parking lot basketball game for later. Perhaps a concerned teacher or parent begins also to see something new in this child in worship that balances their worry about his faithful and challenged growth.

❑ A parishioner gathers the thanksgivings and prayer concerns and weaves together a congregational prayer that leads into the Lord's Prayer. The pastor/preacher realizes that for the first time in weeks she herself has actually been prayerful and not scattered, usually thinking ahead to the sermon during the prayer.

❑ A reading of Luke 8:40-56 involves a narrator and persons to move through the story and say the words of Jesus, Jairus (give him wording for verses 41-42 and 56), Peter, a woman (give her wording for verse 47), a person in the crowd (verse 49), and a young girl. The scripture comes alive for the congregation as they catch a glimpse of what it might have been like to actually be in the healing presence of Jesus. A woman whose husband has been drinking more and starting to demean her when he is drunk is reminded of the care and value Jesus placed on women and takes courage. A young girl is reminded about her father's care for her when she was sick and is thankful.

Notice that these descriptions not only express how a gift is used in worship but also how participation and thus worship is increased in the congregation or in individuals. It is a reminder that congregational participation also happens in the pews and around the table, praying together, singing together, being engaged in listening or thinking together, all of which are important for worship together.

Summary

Beginning where we are means different things for pastors, worship leaders, and members of a congregation—all are necessary and each has different tasks and gifts to share. Believing that the sharing of even three persons' gifts can enhance our worship and make it more authentic and communal, this chapter has encouraged the discernment of the varieties of gifts that can be helpful in planning, preparing, and leading worship. Equipping the use of these gifts is part of the task of pastors and worship leaders, while resource persons, seminaries and colleges, workshops and conferences, or books and videos may be helpful as well. Using the gifts of more of the congregation in worship not only enhances their participation and our sense of community but also brings worship more alive for all of us. Time to look at our worship space in the next chapter!

functioning of worship within a different space. Understanding and working with your space is important for how your community will be shaped by your worship experience.

Essentials

Gordon Lathrop has defined the central things of worship as: "An open and participating community gathered on the Lord's Day in song and prayer around the Scriptures read and preached, around baptismal washing, enacted or remembered, around the holy supper, and around sending to a needy world."[1] In chapter 1 we talked about the worship community that includes and is participatory; in chapters 4 and 5 we will discuss scripture, song and prayer, and planning worship services; in chapter 6, baptism and the supper. Let's look again at this definition to list the essentials for space:
1. A place for the community to gather
2. The centrality of scripture, through reading and preaching
3. The centrality of baptismal washing, either enacted or remembered
4. The centrality of the holy supper, through bread and cup
5. Although worship may be set apart, it sends us out to a needy world.

In the following paragraphs, we will consider how each of these works within the worship experience in a variety of settings: church building—both the right size and too large—storefront or rented building, home, and outdoors. While you may be tempted to jump to one of these sections, there is much overlap, so at least skim through each one to assist your understanding of worship spaces and how they function.

Church Building

Many of you have inherited or built a church building, a building that has shaped your congregation and the perception of the community around it. If you have the privilege of beginning to build or the challenge of space that has been outgrown, you will do well to consider the excellent resource *Church Architecture: Building and Renovating for Christian Worship* by James F. White and Susan J. White.[2] If you have a church building, the following questions can begin discussion about how you are using the space and how its use might be enhanced in your worship together. I will use the word *sanctuary* here, presuming that this is your space; other rooms in a church building may also be used for worship, but they are more like the other spaces we will consider (a fellowship hall is akin to a storefront or rented building, while a church parlor or lounge may be more like worshiping in a house). This first set of questions and possible solutions may be applied whether your worship space is just right or too large:

1. Where is the space for the community to gather before worship—narthex, coatroom, fellowship hall, parking lot, or the sanctuary itself? This has implications for welcoming and for centering times in preparation for worship. Is your space conducive to these two things? If so, great; if not, consider options such as greeters in the parking lot or outside the coatroom for welcoming or even in the sanctuary itself, and then mark the transition from welcoming to worship, for example, including a greeting time in the sanctuary informally, followed by a worshipful greeting from the pastor or liturgist and then a brief prelude or silence for centering and focus.

    a. How is the space defined for the community to gather during worship—pews, chairs, flexible or inflexible seating, facing one direction or in the round? Social science suggests that the best way for participation to occur is when those gathered can see each other and all of the essentials of the worship space (see below for ideas about the pulpit, baptismal font and communion/altar table). In the early church, when the Christian community was meeting in houses, and throughout the Middle Ages, when there were only pews along the sides and backs of the sanctuary for the elderly and pregnant

This may require a large lectern or table for holding the book or an acolyte or other book bearer.
  b. Gracefully lift a smaller Bible at the beginning and end of reading from it.
  c. Read the Gospel in the midst of the congregation, to embody the incarnate Word, Jesus. Other readings might also come from the midst of the congregation.
3. In worship, the baptismal washing, enacted or remembered is central. When I send my students out to observe worship services, this is the element that is most often the hardest for them to find, and indeed in many congregations, impossible unless there is an actual baptism. Yet baptism is our entry into the church, our reminder that we are children of the living God, sealed by the Holy Spirit. Perhaps our lack of enthusiasm and energy for worship is due in part to our forgetfulness about baptism, for if we remember and are reminded of it week by week, our love and passion for God and worship can only grow! What reminders are in your sanctuary of baptism?
  a. Is there a font where people can see it? There are two options for a permanent font in a sanctuary, either by the main entrance to remind us that we enter the church through baptism or on a central axis with the communion table and the pulpit to remind us that baptism and the supper and the Scriptures bind us to Christ. If you have a font or pool, place it where people are reminded of their baptism and where the congregation can gather around it for actual baptisms. (This may help you determine its placement, whether you have more space at the entrance or up front.)
  b. If you do not have a permanent font, consider possibilities for enhancing your worship and faith journey together for including a regular physical reminder of baptism.
    i. If your church is by a river or creek, open the windows occasionally to let its sounds in.

    ii. Install a small fountain of running water at a place in the sanctuary where it may be seen and heard.

   iii. Hang a banner that proclaims a statement reminding people of their baptism and of the work God is doing in their lives or gives thanks for the gifts of water and the Spirit.[4]

   iv. Occasionally highlight a stained-glass window that includes an image of baptism.

    v. Include a reminder of baptism in the opening greeting each week: "Good morning, church"; "Remember that you are baptized"; "Welcome, children of God."

4. Like baptism, the holy supper is central. In early Christianity the breaking of bread (Acts 2:42) was an essential part of worship, and the table had central place. During the Middle Ages, the table and participation in communion became more and more removed from the congregation so that eventually the table was backed up against the farthest wall from the congregation, the priest said the prayer with his back toward the congregation, and very few persons even ate the bread. The Protestant Reformation set out to change our perceptions of communion and restore them to something more like the early church; in the mid-twentieth century, Vatican II and the liturgical renewal movement worked together to suggest that communion tables needed to be where the congregation could gather and where the presider can stand facing the people as she or he leads the prayer. Do you have a communion table in your worship space? Is it placed so that the presider can stand behind it and face the congregation while she or he leads the Great Thanksgiving? Can people gather around the table for receiving the bread and cup? Is it accessible for persons who have trouble climbing steps? Is communion a frequent part of your worship? Is the table so full of things that there is no room for the bread and cup?

5. Finally, how are the needs of the world physically present in the worship space and sending forth? Does some of the artwork represent cultures other than our own? Is there evidence of any

mission outreach in the worship space—offerings of food or collections of blankets? Is our worship space so richly appointed that there is not money left over to share with the world? Is there space for a sense of being sent forth into the world?

In a worship space that is just the right size, there is room for processionals in to worship and out to the world. There is room for the entire congregation to gather around or near the baptismal font. There is room for people to gather around the communion table and stay to pray or leave to return to their seats gracefully. There are good sight lines to where the Scriptures are read and proclaimed. There is enough room for unexpected visitors but not so much that the congregation feels "less than." Baptism, communion, and scripture are all central rather than peripheral to the worshiping community.

In a worship space that is too large, the pews are so empty that singing together is difficult and it is hard for the ushers to pass the offering plates because of the gaps. Similarly, the action in worship all seems far away, up a long aisle in a chancel that only a few persons can enter. Rope off the pews in the back, so that persons will sit toward the front and nearer to their neighbors, or remove one set of the front pews so that there is room to gather together around the baptismal font and communion table. If the space is totally overwhelming yet you don't want to abandon it because memory and grace reside there, try having the congregation sit in the chancel together; through baptism we have all been given access to God and to this holy space. Don't be afraid to make the space fit you until you fit it better.

Storefront or Rental Building

Some may rent space from another church or a movie theater. Others may have temporary or permanent use of office space or storefronts. How can you make the space inviting and holy?

While there is not one physical thing that makes a space holy (God does that!), White and White remind us of several criteria in their book *Church Architecture*. First, "the primary symbol of worship is always the community itself, assembled in Christ's name."[5] The other priority is hospitality, defined by White and White as "space for participation which conveys a sense of intimacy."

Because the people are the primary symbol, be wary of adding too many other symbols that may distract or overwhelm. That being said, we are currently in the pendulum swing in sanctuary design, moving from stark and minimalist (like the sanctuary and building at Willow Creek, which looks like an office building on the outside and has no Christian symbols in its main auditorium) to more "homey" (with some groups actually meeting in living rooms, others opting for the comfort of a local pub or coffee shop, and a trend toward "decoration" of the altar table). Let's move back to Lathrop's essentials to see how they might be translated for a congregation worshiping in a storefront or rented building.

1. A place for the community to gather. How does gathering happen in this place? Is it welcoming? In order to provide space for participation that conveys a sense of intimacy, try to reserve or rent a room that is adjustable to your congregation's size or slightly larger than the needed seating and gathering space. If you are providing chairs, consider a rocking chair or two for parents with children or someone with back problems. You may also need to "clear away" the evidence of the former life of the space. Will there be any instrument to accompany or pitch the singing?

    a. Does the space need warming up with paint, fabric, or lighting? Working together on a space that is permanent or has "landlord permission" to paint and refloor (carpet, tile, rugs) can be a good project to bring your worship group together. Make sure there is adequate lighting for those who will be reading or playing instruments, especially if you are in a theater, which is made for darkness rather than light. Make sure that lighting is adjustable if you are using projected media in nontheater space.

    b. If you have secular space, you may have the advantage of pulling in persons who avoid "churchy" buildings. But then you have the challenge of making the space holy, not simply where Alcoholics Anonymous or the local civic club might meet. Whether you are using temporary or permanent space, it will be important for your congregation to bring some things that mark the space as holy for you together.

c. Just as constant business travelers bring a picture of family and a special object along for their nightstand in the hotel, so a "traveling congregation" might want to bring some things to use in borrowed space to make it your own. Have a discussion or two about what symbolizes your worship together. Is it a cross, candlesticks, some colorful fabric to drape for the liturgical season, communion vessels, or a special banner? Do you want something that has been created or commissioned by members of your worshiping group?[6]

2. The centrality of scripture, through reading and preaching. Often you will need to bring a Bible into your rented or borrowed space. What size of Bible will signify the importance it holds for your congregation while not being too heavy to lift? Or do you want a lectern, pulpit, or desk to assist in holding a large or heavy Bible when it is being read from? If persons will be sitting around tables, do you simply need a book stand to hold the Bible? Do you want the Word to be read and proclaimed from the midst of the worshiping congregation? Groups of up to fifteen or twenty persons may decide to be seated in a circle or around a table and not feel the need for a pulpit or lectern, choosing instead to use a standard-sized Bible to read from and talking together about the scripture and its application for their lives.[7] Groups over twenty persons may feel the need for a more clearly marked location for reading and proclaiming the Word; either bringing or storing a lectern for the worship space will be important.

3. The centrality of baptismal washing, enacted or remembered. Groups using borrowed or rented space may be challenged for baptismal space because any font that holds a significant

amount of water will be heavy to move in and out of temporary space. You might want to consider using a local lake or river for baptisms, meeting that day at the site; in that case you might consider having a banner, small running fountain, or other representation of water/river (be creative!) to use weekly in your worship space.[8] Or, you may find that creating or commissioning a baptismal font that is moveable and has been specially made for your congregation is a rich symbol to include in your worship space every week.

4. The centrality of the holy supper, through bread and cup. In storefront or rented space, you may well want to follow the custom of some of the early Reformed churches of setting out tables surrounded by enough chairs for everyone, conducting worship around the tables. Having the congregation's own chalices and patens for the wine/juice and bread is important; if someone in the congregation wants to make these, resources and models are available, such as Hoyt Hickman's *United Methodist Altars: A Guide for the Local Church*. Many churches of three to ninety-nine people find that communion is important for them to celebrate every week, and so they find different ways to celebrate: eating together, around tables, gathering in a circle and then serving one another, or gathering together around an altar table.[9] Even if you don't celebrate communion every week, you may wish to include an altar table in your worship space to remind the congregation of how Christ feeds us and forgives us constantly.

5. Sending to a needy world. It may be that the reason your worshiping circle is meeting in a storefront is that you have a ministry to the neighborhood at that location. If so, great—you have natural and organic ways to connect with the needy world, including symbols and representations of the ministry that goes on in that space. If not, the possible solutions to represent the world and our being sent include, as it did within church buildings: artwork that represents cultures other than our own, evidence of mission outreach in the worship space—offerings of food or collections of blankets—and space for being sent forth into the world.

One thing to consider for churches that are meeting in storefronts or other rented or borrowed space is the stewardship of this practice. Many churches get caught up in their buildings, and it is easy to see why—a church building is a visible reminder in the world of the presence of God; it is distinctive and thus easy for people to find; the permanence of the space lends itself to liberated and creative use of that space; it is easier to raise donations for a building that people can see than ministry programs that they can't always see; and in a congregation whose primary function together is worship, the sanctuary becomes a place of memory and holiness. Yet, there are drawbacks to owning a building that takes all the money you can raise just to keep it in running order, to worrying more about the building than about your ministry, to going into debt for something that the next generation may find outdated or cumbersome. Many worshiping groups of up to one hundred persons might find that using borrowed or rented space frees them to support a full-time pastor and more ministry options. It is worth considering these options as you try to be the best stewards you can of the resources God has given you.

Meeting in a Home

Considering concerns about stewardship of resources mentioned in the previous section, some worshiping groups might choose to meet temporarily or permanently in the home of a member. This resonates with the practice of early churches and poses opportunities and challenges of its own.[10]

1. A place for the community to gather. Return to White and White's priorities of hospitality, participation, and intimacy. Communities worshiping in homes have a natural advantage with more intimate spaces; their challenges are hospitality and participation.

      a. First, this means finding people or families who are hospitable and comfortable having other people in their home once a week or on a rotation. In North

America many of us are more private and think that hosting persons in our homes means certain standards of housekeeping and interior decoration. Since we are using the Gospel as our standard and not "Lifestyles of the Rich and Famous," we need to be consistent in discussions with each other about our worshiping space.

b. Another challenge in meeting in someone's home is finding a space that will accommodate all of the worshipers comfortably; it does no good to have persons thinking, "Well, they will be less crowded if I don't go today." So these hosts need to have space (living room, great room, family room, basement space, patio, or outdoor space[11]) that can hold your current worshiping group and room for a few friends.

c. Like those for borrowed or owned spaces, the requirements for gathering in homes include: entrance space that is accessible, places for coats or rain gear, seating or comfortable floor space that also has enough room for movement as desired, space for the symbols of baptism and communion (see below), adequate lighting, without decoration that will distract from the worship experience.

2. The centrality of scripture, through reading and preaching. There is something incongruous about sitting in someone's living room with a dozen or so people and then setting up a podium or pulpit for someone to stand and preach from. Instead, this space suggests scripture reading in the midst of the gathered folks, standing if that helps the hearing and sight lines (for some, being able to see the reader/preacher helps them hear, even if they don't read lips). It suggests preaching that is done in the style of Luke 4:16-20, as Jesus followed the synagogue tradition of the time by standing to read the scripture that was given to him but sitting to interpret it.

The Bible is still important and to be honored, so use it in ways that are respectful; the size of it within the house will not need to be other than standard because the scale is smaller here than in a church and the intimacy doesn't require the more significantly sized Bible that a storefront might.

3. The centrality of baptismal washing, enacted or remembered. This can be a challenging point for communities worshiping in a home. Do not use the bathroom, however luxurious it is.

    a. If there is a pool, care will need to be taken to distinguish a baptism from the after-worship swim; the after-worship swim can remind us of our baptism, but it is not the same. Wearing special clothes, by the candidate and the person leading the baptism, can help; baptismal robes, shaped like choir or pastoral robes, are traditionally white and have weights sewn into their hems to prevent them from floating up. In the urban early church, after up to three years of study and practice, persons would be baptized at dawn on Easter; daybreak may help set the mood, and candles and appropriate music can also assist. Transition from the baptism by singing a hymn and moving back into the worship space while the candidate changes into worship clothes; then continue worship, rather than moving right into an open swim.

    b. If you are meeting in a space without a pool, you may wish to borrow another congregation's worship space that includes a baptismal font or pool. When traveling to this other space that is more conducive to baptism, you lose the natural weekly reminder of your baptism. So take something that you use regularly in worship—a cross or banner—to the borrowed space and include something in your regular worship space to remind you of baptism.[12]

    c. Another option when you are meeting in homes is to move to a lake or river when baptizing.[13] Again, this has the heightened experience of something new but the disadvantage of breaking the link with weekly worship. Here you might bridge the gap back to your worship in someone's home by taking a picture of the river or lake or of the baptized, enlarging it and framing it as a visual reminder.

d. Another easy way to remember your baptism in weekly worship in someone's home is to have a special small running fountain that is set up each week within your space or to have a bowl and pitcher in blues or water tones sitting each week within your space. Reaffirmations of baptism are very appropriate for congregations meeting in homes and simply need enough space to move around in, so that persons can either move to the water or the water can pass to them.

4. The centrality of the holy supper, through bread and cup. This can be particularly intensified within a group meeting in someone's home because it has the resonance of Jesus' and the disciples' meeting in the upper room of someone's home to celebrate this meal.

a. If there is dining or kitchen space available (or picnic tables outside) that can fit your entire worshiping group, this space can be ideal. Let the presider sit at one end of the table where everyone can see her or him, then pass the bread and cup and serve each other. Leaving a time for silence at the end, where you pray for one another and for the world that God loves, can be particularly meaningful.

b. If you are worshiping in a living room, den, or family room, clear the space either for a serving station at a communion table where all can move for receiving or place a table in the middle of a circle and then serve each other around the table while standing or sitting (someone will probably have to move within and among people if you are seated).

c. If you have worship without communion, consider what will remind the community of that gift. Will you set up an altar table at one end of the worshiping space or in the middle? Will you put a chalice and paten on it? Will there be a visual reminder of worship outdoors, where "living" water is readily available. Make certain that the water is clean and safe and that people are prepared for its use. Baptizing in a lake or river may awaken people's fears about water, so be pastoral and adapt as needed for the individual candidates for baptism.

    a. If you are baptizing in a river, beware of any currents in rainy times and any drying up during times of drought, as well as slippery river beds or rocks. It may take two persons for baptizing if the current is strong, and a cup or lightweight pitcher to assist with pouring water over the head if you can stand in the water but not "go under." (See additional methods below.) Consider having special baptismal robes or clothes for the candidates for baptism and the leaders, garments that are weighted as needed and thick when wet. Towels are appropriate, as is a place to change for the rest of the service and appropriate assistance in doing so. There are plenty of lovely baptismal hymns for congregations to sing while those who are wet are changing.

    b. If you are baptizing in a lake or ocean, beware of slippery ocean floors or rocks, of the danger of contracting "swimmer's itch" from the water, of any sudden drop-offs, or of a strong undertow. Depending on the height of the presider and the candidates, a sponsor or assistant may be helpful. Traditions vary over whether the candidate:

        i. stands knee-deep or waist-deep in the water and has additional water poured over the head (see Renaissance and Sunday school pictures of Jesus baptized this way),

        ii. kneels in waist-deep water and is taken forward so that their whole body is briefly underwater; both i and ii work well with persons who have fears of drowning,[15] though it may not work as well if there is a current or undertow,

    iii. stands in waist-deep or higher water and is taken either forward or backward by the presider and assistant or sponsor, or

    iv. is dipped once or three times—some say three times in honor of the Trinity, but in the current state in North America where we have occasionally trifurcated the Trinity,[16] once may be more symbolic, especially if it is done slowly and with grace.

4. The centrality of the holy supper, through bread and cup. An altar table is useful but not essential, as long as the elements are handled with respect. Picnic tables to sit around would be appropriate. Otherwise, gathering around an altar table or even in a circle to pass the elements also works; the circle needs to be small enough so that voices will carry as needed. You may wish to cover the bread and wine/juice with white linen cloths when outside to keep bugs out and also add to the respect for the elements. This is also the time to remember that you will most likely be worshiping without bulletins or projected screens, so use responses that people know by heart or songs that are a part of the common repertoire. If there are winds, make sure that the communion elements and their coverings are well anchored.

5. Sending to a needy world. Although worship may be set apart, it sends us to a needy world. Worshiping in the outdoors can definitely give us the sense of being set apart and in a holy place. Being sent into a needy world does not have to be difficult, though. Make certain that the needy world finds its way into your prayers. And, occasionally make leaving worship a processional, down the mountain, up from the valley, to the parking lot or cabins from the waterfront, a processional with singing and energy and commissioning for service to the world.

Summary

In this chapter we have considered opportunities and challenges of worship settings—in churches just right and those too

Working Alone or Planning Together

One of the biases of this book is that worship is better when it involves everyone in using their gifts for the glory of God. But perhaps you are the pastor or worship leader whose congregation thinks that worship is your responsibility, not theirs. For now, you might use the processes in this chapter on your own, knowing that it is a step on the journey to something else. That something else might start either of two ways.

First, if there is one person in the congregation who seems interested in worship, either stepping up to read a scripture, seeing that everyone has a bulletin, or giving you positive facial feedback in worship, ask that person to meet with you "just to talk." Share some of the ideas from the first chapter in this book; see where there is affirmation; ask if this person would be willing to meet with you once a month to discuss worship in your congregation; start with just a few questions: *What are the most essential traditions in this congregation and why do you think they are important to persons here? Is there someone who is a good storyteller? Who loves to decorate at Christmas? If you were ill, who in the worshiping community would you want praying for you? I found this brief drama that illustrates something I'm going to preach about next month—what do you think? Is there anyone who might help do this?* Slowly gathering even two or three persons for coffee and discussion will assist you to know the congregation better, get some feedback, and begin to widen the circle of support for your work. Some pastors find that a Bible study or prayer group is a natural fit for some of this work; taking ten minutes of the group's time to look at or pray over a scripture for an upcoming worship can yield important insights for you and begin to prepare the group's hearts for worship. Some worship leaders find their support for this work in a choir or band or altar guild. Don't let yourself as pastor or worship leader feel that worship planning is a burden— find dialogue partners!

Second, if it really seems that there is no one currently in your worshiping congregation who is willing to discuss worship with you (although you may need to find out why, then, they come to worship!), look for other pastors or worship leaders for dialogue partners. Some pastors or worship leaders find it useful to gather with colleagues from seminary or pastors' school for an afternoon or retreat day to plan worship for the upcoming months. Others may find that an ecumenical ministers' group provides for lectionary Bible study, a combined worship service, or simply "talk time" about worship. Many denominations and seminaries have workshops on preaching and worship that can inspire and equip you; look for dialogue partners there as well. If you are the worship leader for your congregation, you have a duty to God and to yourself to "keep your pump primed" by going to the well of God's love through the Christian community as often as you can. Even if you don't get ideas for week-by-week worship, you will get one or two for something upcoming, and that will be enough because you know there are others working for God in their own places just as you are.

Focus: Lectionary Scripture, Liturgical Season, or Theological Theme

In order for worship to be a convergence and still be accessible to human minds, hearts, and bodies, it is important for the various elements to fit together. For the impact of worship and its lodging in our memory, focusing on a particular scripture, season, or theme is vital.

Lectionary

Many worshiping communities use what is known as a lectionary, a list of scripture readings for each worship time, to guide their worship. In Luke 4:17, visiting the synagogue in Nazareth, Jesus is handed the scroll of the prophet Isaiah. Notice that he doesn't ask for this particular scroll; it is handed to him because it is the set reading for the day, demonstrating the use of a lectionary even in early times. Currently many Christian communities use *The Revised Common Lectionary,* a set of scripture readings assigned over a three-year cycle to cover a significant portion of the Bible in those three years.[1] *The Revised Common Lectionary* contains four readings for each day—Hebrew Bible, Psalm, Epistle, and Gospel—focusing on Matthew in Year A, Mark in Year B, Luke in Year C, with John's gospel scattered throughout the three years. Using the lectionary enhances our worship in several ways:

1. We are not left to our own devices in planning or at the whim of the particular passages we love or think this congregation needs to hear. Much of the Bible is covered over each three-year cycle, including some of the "hard" passages we might be tempted to ignore.

2. There are many worship resources that are built around *The Revised Common Lectionary*—scripture studies, hymn selections, suggestions for focus and visual art, bulletin covers, and some very helpful websites such as www.textweek.com. This makes using the lectionary for worship planning very useful when involving a team effort rather than everyone waiting for the worship leader or pastor to "receive inspiration."

3. The presence of the Spirit works through the lectionary in wonderful ways. During the weeks after September 11, 2001, the Hebrew Bible readings in the lectionary were from the book of Jeremiah, full of lament that matched the grieving of many people. Pastors and worship leaders have often found that the readings that they looked at a month ago suddenly have new significance for their congregation or community.

4. The lectionary is in tune with the seasons of the liturgical year and thus helps to give a rhythm to our life together. This does not mean that once we start using the lectionary we are locked into it forever; some congregations may decide over the summer to focus on a particular epistle or prophetic reading. Others may wish to take a month to talk about a particular issue that is important and pressing in their community. Look at the lectionary first to see if it speaks to this issue; if not, search for other scriptures that do.

The Liturgical Year

Focusing on the seasons of the liturgical year is another way to plan worship. Notice that this is different than focusing on the seasons of the secular world; it is very tempting to get caught up in Christmas shopping and Santa in December, but it is the task of the church to remind us that God's time is different than human time, God's focus different than human focus.

The liturgical year is organized around the two major events of the life of Jesus, his incarnation (Christmas) and his death and resurrection (Good Friday and Easter). Each of these holy days is preceded by a season of preparation (Advent and Lent, respectively) and followed by a secondary holy day (Epiphany and Pentecost). Between the secondary days and the next season of preparation we have "ordinary days" when we hear of Jesus' ministries of teaching, healing, and feeding, which are actually extraordinary events.

Human life is centered on rhythms and seasons of life—birth, death, birthdays, weddings, anniversaries, beginnings of school and work, endings of relationships, jobs, and school years. The liturgical year reminds us that God's time envelopes our time, and it gives us a shape for celebrating our own place within God's time. By the wonders of creation and time, the liturgical year also reminds us that the God who entered human history in the form of Jesus Christ is also Creator and Lord of the universe; the incarnation cycle is based on the solar cycle with the set calendar date of December 25, whereas the Easter cycle is based on the lunar cycle with a movable date. Within this yearly and cosmic cycle, we gather together every seven days, weekly, to worship God who holds the universe, time, and us in hand.

Focusing on a season or holy day may mean that your planning studies the history of All Saints' Day and looks for historic prayers around its twin themes of those who have lived holy lives and died and those who are trying to live holy lives here and now. During Lent, it may mean studying the prayers found in scripture and learning some of the many ways throughout history that Christians have found to pray. Or, it may simply mean that while following the lectionary scriptures as your basis for worship, you highlight a particular color or art form or worship gift during a season of the liturgical year.

Theological Theme

Focusing worship around a theological theme takes more work simply because most worship resources are organized around scripture/lectionary or the liturgical year. However, there are resources available around themes such as forgiveness, creation, incarnation, stewardship, and so on, both online and in book or DVD form. Themed worship works best on a limited-time basis—either as a single worship experience (for example, a homecoming service that focuses on Christian community or thanksgiving to God) or a month-long series of services (for example, on forgiveness, with each of the four weeks devoted to a facet of forgiveness: sin/trespass/debt, the work of Jesus Christ in forgiveness, forgiving one another, living as forgiven and redeemed people).

For worship around a theological theme, a pastor can recommend a book for study, and then work would be done with a Bible concordance for appropriate scriptures and hymnal indices or online searches for appropriate music. Websites such as www.text week.com also have links to artwork and appropriate films for theological themes as well as seasons and the lectionary.

The Creative Process

Once you know what direction the worship time is based on and headed in, you are ready to engage in a creative process. For some of you, this process may well be part of your discernment about the focus of the worship experience, for others the choice of focus will be given to you by previous choice of lectionary use or by a pastor or worship leader.

Following the pattern outlined in Ruth Duck's *Finding Words for Worship* (chapter 2, "The Creative Process"):[2]

1. Begin with prayer. Whether you are working alone or with other persons, this frames your work in the best way.

2. Engage your imagination, letting images from the scripture and daily life speak. What does this text or event look like? Sound like? Smell like? Feel like? Taste like? Does it have movement? If it is an ancient or historic event or text, is there a modern-day parallel?

3. Brainstorm ideas, writing them down either in clusters of similar ideas or scraps of paper. In this step there are no "wrong" ideas; generate as many as possible, knowing that you will only use a few for this particular service (so save the others for the next time you consider that scripture or event). Focus on the ideas that will engage your congregation with this scripture or event. There are several ways of prioritizing your choices:

    a. Focus on a new way of considering this scripture or human experience.

    b. Focus on an idea that allows development through some of the congregational gifts for worship that you discerned in chapter 2.

    c. Focus on the heart of the gospel—which ideas get us closer to that?

    d. Focus on the issues that are tempting to avoid, but though hard, may be exactly the ones we need to focus on.

4. Let your work flow: pick music, words for prayers, visuals, and sermon ideas without censoring yourself. Editing is not in this step; it will come later; the flow of words and choices around art and music and activities happens now.

5. Take time away—a day or two is best, but even a coffee/tea break or short walk will assist you in returning to your work with a fresh mind.

6. Revise and edit. Make sure that all that you are doing "sticks like glue" to your main focus (#4 above). Be open and humble to taking things out and including more appropriate things. Edit to your heart's content within whatever time limits you have. Remember the only perfect worship experience will be in heaven!

7. Learn from feedback. Listen with your ears, eyes, and heart as your work is brought to life. Watch for persons' involvement; get their feedback so that your work will continue to improve. If you are in a formal feedback situation (small feedback group, survey, or even one-on-one) remember that it takes about five positive things to balance each negative. So ask for positive things first and keep track of them. At the least, ask for three things that persons found "helpful" and one thing they might change. If you set up a regular feedback group, through careful work and trust and visible improvement, that balance may be relaxed.

8. Give thanks for the opportunity to work with God's people and the things of God through worship. And then on to the next task!

A Word about Adapting

You have already heard in this text the use of the word *adapt* with discussion about worship gifts and in taking home materials from a worship conference or class. Since it is such an important task of all worship leaders, let's look at it more closely.

To *adapt* means that there is something there already—maybe a written prayer, a song, a space, a skit, choreography, a litany. When you as a worship planning team or worship leader look at this resource, ask yourself several questions:

1. Is this appropriate for our particular worship experience, its scripture and theme? If it is just beautiful and the answer to the question is no, file it away for another experience.

2. Does the language resonate with the "heart language" of our worshiping community? Whereas using other language families (Spanish, Swahili, and so forth) is important for diversity, this question really addresses the spiritual language and dialect of your particular community. The King James Version of the Bible is heart language for some congregations, but, in others, it would seem like a foreign language; those congregations might claim *The New Revised Standard Version of the Bible* or *The Message* Bible

as their heart language. A movie or television show that is mentioned in a drama you are considering might not mean anything either to the median age of your congregation or to your area; maybe it's an independent film that never played in your theater or a cable show that never gets watched because everyone is at the local high school for Friday night football. Check the language for slang or other expressions that your congregation might find offensive or confusing, especially when you are drawing from more secular resources.

3. Are there words that would need defining for this worshiping community? If you are trying to teach people the language of worship and theology, then include a definition immediately. For example, if the introduction to a drama said, "This incident is based on a pericope of the Bible," add to define: "This incident is based on a pericope, *or set of verses*, of the Bible." Other words that may need defining include *salvation, redemption, eschatology, apocrypha,* or biblical images such as Gideon's fleece or the widow's mite.[3] If the word is simply a large word, then use the meaning instead of the large word; for example, for *quadruped,* you would substitute *four-legged.* If the word is something that is foreign to your congregation, find a way to demonstrate it if that aids in diversity and metaphor; for example, bring in a plumb line when basing worship on Amos 7. You may need to recontextualize, that is, find another word or metaphor that your congregation will understand; for example, Tim Ladwig's *Psalm 23* is a simple and wonderful example of recontextualizing, which uses pictures to put the psalm into an urban environment for children.[4]

4. Is there a way to personalize this resource for our congregation? If it is a prayer of thanksgiving with a lot of rural metaphors and your congregation is inner-city, take the form of the prayer and add your own thanks using more urban metaphors. If the drama mentions a restaurant, make it a local one. If you are working on a prayer, creed, or litany, include ways of naming grace or lament that your congregation will understand and resonate with.

5. Is there anything that will be hard for persons to hear or that will need to be nuanced so that it might be heard? Consider the

scripture praising laying down your life (John 15:13)—in a congregation where a youth has recently attempted suicide; the context where Jesus is preparing to lay down his life for his friends is very different. On Good Friday, care with the abuse aspects of the story in any congregation where abuse happens (and that would be many of our congregations) means that we focus not on human degradation but on Jesus' willingness to sacrifice, his great love, and his graciousness to persons nearby (his mother, the repentant thief). The challenge may be the scriptural challenges to rich and poor, powerful and oppressed—let the scripture speak its truth and also pray for ways to assist that speaking with deep love.

All of these ways of adapting mean paying attention to your particular worshiping community and its daily life outside the worship time. It means knowing and loving the people who come to worship with you, and it means working with God so that God's message may be heard and seen and felt. The next chapter moves us into the fourfold shape of worship and actual planning.

Planning the Actual Service

When he came to Nazareth, where he had been brought up, [Jesus] went to the synagogue on the sabbath day, as was his custom. He stood up to read, and the scroll of the prophet Isaiah was given to him. (Luke 4:16-17a)

The Fourfold Shape of Worship

While worship through the centuries has had distinctive texts and settings, music and movement, the basic shape of it has remained consistently fourfold:

1. Gathering: Greeting each other and newcomers in the name of God, centering ourselves and our community through song, prayer, and silence
2. Hearing the Word: The reading of scripture, preaching, interpretations of the Word in music, visual art, movement, or drama
3. Responding to the Word: Through thanksgiving and offering, in baptism or affirmation of faith, through communion, through prayer and song
4. Sending forth: In mission, with blessing

In different traditions, there may be an emphasis or more time given to one area of this shape. In the revival pattern of worship, which grew out of camp meetings on the frontier and revival meetings in the tradition of Dwight Moody and Ira Sankey, Charles Finney, and Billy Graham, the gathering time gained momentum toward the preaching of the Word and culminated ultimately in the response of conversion. In praise and worship patterns, the gathering time may take up to two-thirds of the time of the worship experience, with brief time for response or sending forth. In liturgical churches, the response to the Word in communion may be the central focus of the service. In worship that is commissioning persons to go on a mission trip, the sending forth may be the highlight. Brad Berglund calls the pattern: Gathering, Encountering, Responding, and Embracing.[1]

As you read the following steps for planning the worship experience, know that while this process may look daunting and complicated, there is variation in how long each step will take, in part, due to your level of practice in worship planning. The longer you do this, the more natural and less tedious the steps will seem. The planning time will not automatically shorten because planning wonderful worship experiences can take time, but you will find it an energizing and productive process that leads you into new ways of looking at the convergence of God, worship, and your community.

If you are feeling overwhelmed at beginning this process, give it an occasional try, perhaps for Christmas Eve, which has become so "traditional" that it no longer speaks for some, or for another special service such as Thanksgiving or Homecoming. Or, perhaps pick just one change to make—it will make a difference.

Then gather a group to plan for a season—Advent or Lent or the Great Fifty Days all lend themselves to intentional worship and work together with reasonable amounts of time, natural seasonal foci, and scriptures. Rotating the planning group can also energize the leaders and help to make worship more the work of all the congregation, and the "workshop of Christian life together" will remind you not to make these groups or your worship competitive but to do all to build each other up so that God may be glorified (Ephesians 4:12).

Every worshiping group should have a library of resources for planning and enhancing the worship experience. At a minimum, this library should include a good study Bible, your denomination's worship book and at least one other denomination's worship book, your hymnal, the hymnal companion, a good book on visual art or symbolism for worship, and access to the internet. (If internet access is not possible at your location, you can try your local public library.) Appendix 2, "Resources: A Sample Basic Worship Library," gives suggestions with some annotations to guide you in gathering these resources, both in print and online. More on the use of the arts in worship will be found in chapter 7.

Hearing the Word

Begin your planning by determining how the Word will be heard and proclaimed in this particular worship experience. This means consideration of not only the reading of scripture and preaching but also interpretations of the Word through music, visual art, movement, or drama. We often begin planning worship with the Gathering and use up our best energies on that; beginning with the Word is not only more appropriate in framing and focusing our worship but also guarantees that this part of the worship experience will be given adequate consideration.

If you began your work with the lectionary, your scripture choices have a natural limitation, and now is the time to apply the creative process to what will be your focus scripture or even a focus verse. Once you begin to look carefully at scripture and apply your imagination, you will realize that often one verse alone will supply multiple themes and ideas for worship; just be aware that if you focus on one verse, you have allowed its context in the whole passage to shape its meaning for you; taking scripture out of its context may yield misinterpretations.

If you began your work with a liturgical season, you may have found things coalescing about a scripture related to that time. If so, proceed to the next steps. If not, there are two primary ways to choose a related scripture. First, you might check a lectionary for that season or holy day and focus on one of the suggested scriptures; lectionaries may be found in books of worship or online (such as www.textweek.com). Second, you might use a Bible concordance (a large book with scriptures listed for each major word in the Bible) or "word search" on computer Bible; in these resources you might look up words like *thanks* or *thanksgiving,* or *spirit* or *heal.* Again, pay attention to the verses around your chosen verse(s), so that you don't take anything out of context.

If you began your work with a theological theme, you may find scriptures in your study book, a Bible concordance, or through a word search on computer Bible, looking up your primary words or variations on them.[2] The computer is an incredible resource for thematic worship, but be careful that you use discernment with the resources that you choose—the internet has many trustworthy resources, but it also has things that are very biased and do not use scripture or theology in careful and thoughtful ways; just because it is posted on the internet does not mean it is true. Test whatever you find against your own knowledge of scripture and the criteria of building up the kin-dom of God by following the great commandments of loving God and our neighbor with all of our being.

In all this work, you are looking for central words, themes, images, and metaphors that will express the faith of your worshiping community to God and also shape that faith more deeply and broadly. Metaphors work by providing tension between two things that are relatively similar (is) but also very different (is not); in this tension we can see truth in new ways, not all of them expressible in words. To say that "God is a rock" is not to say that all rocks have God in them, or that God is cold and hard; it is a metaphor that proclaims that one of the ways we know God is by God's similarities to the firmness and sureness of a mighty rock, and through the spiritual "My God is a rock in a weary land" we sense the ability to lean against God's sureness when we are unsure and shifting. Discovering a key metaphor, which will have an is/is not tension, can provide an energetic core to your worship experience, and thus your planning.

Now you are ready to work with "hearing the Word." Planning this way reminds us that the proximity of scripture reading and the message is important. How will the Scripture be read—by the preacher or liturgist or another layperson? (Note that if you are focusing on a theological theme you may be using a second reading from a study book; that can be very appropriate and edifying, but it doesn't replace at least one reading from the Bible.) Will the reading take place at a front location or in the midst of the congregation? Does the scripture lend itself to being read as a dramatic reading, with narrator and different voices?[3] Should some of the secondary voices be placed elsewhere in the worship space? Are there any words in the passage that are difficult to pronounce? If so, get assistance from the pastor or a Bible that includes pronunciation symbols. For some passages it may be helpful to check a map or chronology or family tree to contextualize the place, event, or person. Is the passage a listing of things to do or names, or is it, like some of the epistles, a string of clauses? If so, then make certain that the reading is paced to aid understanding. Are there words in the passage that may be new to people, a theological or biblical concept that might need to be explained? Consider making that explanation part of the children's sermon, if that would be appropriate, or the regular sermon or a bulletin note or PowerPoint slide. What version of the scripture is closest to the heart language of this worshiping community? Do they need to hear it in a different version for a change or challenge?

What theme or focus has the preacher chosen to proclaim in the sermon? Over the years I have met preachers who prefer to read their scripture for the week on Monday and then let the sermon percolate until Friday or even Saturday before settling on a title and focus. I've also met preachers who work ahead three to six weeks, letting the scripture live in them and then as soon as a theme or focus emerges, sharing that with other worship planners, writing the sermon over the week. Although some may be concerned that they will lose focus on the scripture for the week using this second method, it is my experience that it provides for more unified and thus stronger worship experiences, doesn't cause moments of panic for the preacher, gives the Holy Spirit time to work, and celebrates the variety of scripture living within oneself.

One of the advantages of worshiping groups of three to ninety-nine is the opportunity that is automatically present to draw people into a scripture discussion, otherwise known as the message. This is not to say that the preacher abdicates her or his responsibility, but it is to change that responsibility slightly. In what Laurence Wagley called "participatory preaching," the preacher does some exegesis of the scripture for the day and provides background and leading questions for a communal discussion of the scripture passage.[4] The congregation is responsible for input and engagement and for struggling with the application of the scripture to their daily lives. For preachers who are accustomed to proclamation, it may occasionally be challenging to let the congregation find their own voice and not to guide them overly much to what the preacher perceives about the scripture. But, if you are a preacher who believes that all Christians have a responsibility to follow the Word in their daily lives and that God has given us free will in order to work out our salvation (Philippians 2:12-13), there can be no greater joy than facilitating that practice and guiding persons to more wholesome and truthful interpretations of scripture. Start gradually, asking a "nonrhetorical" question in the midst of a message, beginning to prompt response and engagement from the worshiping community. Or, frame this element of the worship experience as "hearing the Word together," sit down with the congregation, make the space safe where there are "no wrong answers" just "more questions waiting to be asked," and jump into discussion.

As an alternative to a preaching message, consider this fact: one of the most popular worshiping communities for persons ages fourteen to thirty in Europe is the Community of Taizé, where the scripture readings during morning, noon, and evening prayer are followed by seven to twelve minutes of silence; only on Friday evenings is there any sort of message. This silence is one reason that many youth give for their appreciation of worship at Taizé, the ability to be alone with their own thoughts about scripture and God while surrounded by others doing likewise. Following the Reformed and revival traditions, most North American Protestants are accustomed to hearing a message or sermon during worship; some persons will raise concern if the message is not sufficient or is done through drama or music. But occasionally providing time for persons to meditate on a scripture without guiding them can begin to give each person the responsibility and the privilege of learning to listen for God's voice in the midst of life. There can be no better place to practice this listening than in the midst of other Christians seeking after the same thing.

Consider how the Word might be heard through music or visual art, through other senses than hearing text. Is there a song text that comes to mind when you are reading the scripture for the day? Hymn and song texts also may be selected by using hymnal indices (there are ones for both scripture and topic at the back of most hymnals), a hymnal concordance (a book like a Bible concordance, arranged by major words from the songs in one particular hymnal), or doing a word search on the internet. (Follow the cautions noted above about use of the internet.) What visual art might be included in the worship space or through projection? Here again, there are resources by scripture (a beautiful and diverse collection of visuals around scriptures may be found in the three volumes of *Imaging the Word: An Arts and Lectionary Resource*) and theme (your worship library or online). Liturgical dancers and dramatists will be able to resource movement and dramas that express the scripture or theme of the day.

As you gather elements for this section of the worship experience, use the creative process to brainstorm, focus, and then place these elements in order. The progression may either take the minds and hearts of the worshipers logically, inductively, or deductively, with one thing leading naturally into the next, or you may use the principle of juxtaposition.[5] Another way of looking at metaphor, juxtaposition works to enliven and challenge our worship. For example, the holy meal is juxtaposed with the sending to a needy world, reminding us of the hunger of the world in light of our being fed; the birth of Jesus is juxtaposed, that is, held in tension, with his death and resurrection, and thus becomes more than simply a sentimental event. While a metaphor captures that tension in a simple phrase, juxtaposition works by placing elements of worship or ideas next to each other and giving time and space for the worshipers to realize the significance for themselves.

Response to the Word

As you work with the scripture and focus of the worship experience, you will begin to generate some ideas about what sort of responses would be appropriate for the Word as it has been proclaimed. Some possible responses are thanksgiving, offering, baptism, affirmation of faith, communion, prayer, song, or an activity either individually or with a group.

If the Word is a proclamation of Good News, the worship experience might include time for individual testimonies or collective thanksgivings related to the scripture. Stories of creation might bring forth naming of favorite elements and places within God's creation; readings from the Epistles that include the opening or closing benedictions might call for similar words of greeting, thanks, and blessing for persons related to your community. Thanksgiving can also be expressed through participation in communion, as the prayer at the table is called the Great Thanksgiving.

Good News may call forth the response of conversion and turning around, which might be expressed through baptism, the remembrance of baptism, or in a prayer for commitment. Other Good News may call for a reaffirmation of faith, recitation of a creed, or singing a hymn or song that affirms belief.

Offerings may be monetary gifts, materials that have been brought to share with the poor or with a mission project, or a joyful dance or song from the congregation. In some cultures, the offering time becomes a joyful procession, as persons come forward to the worship center bringing their thanks and gifts to God with singing or clapping. Other times our offering may be more solemn—turning over a worry into God's keeping, trusting a sin into God's mercy so that we may no longer commit it, or pledging a gift that will be used for God in the coming week (a gift of hospitality, kindness, a skill that we will share); any of these might be accompanied with a promissory note in an offering plate or by procession to an altar table. Consider that collecting the offering is an easy place to involve persons in worship leadership, pairing newcomers with a veteran or a child with a parent or mentor.

The Word may lead a worshiping community to craft letters to a public official about a social concern or to commit to working with a group like Habitat for Humanity[6] or Bread for the World[7] or taking an extra offering to support an animal with the Heifer Project.[8] Cards might be signed for a shut-in's birthday, letters of encouragement sent to prisoners,[9] or pen pal letters for a local elementary school. A discussion may be held to decide how to answer a question raised by the scripture—what will we do about the hungry in our neighborhood?—with some possible steps that people could do over the next month.

Prayer time and silence can be part of a response to the Word, both individually and collectively. A sermon on the prodigal son might be followed with the suggestion to see oneself as the prodigal—what do you need to do to come home to God? Or, another time to see yourself as the father in the story—whom do you need to welcome back or forgive? Or, yet another time to see yourself as the older brother—where does your heart need to be opened to realize all that you have so you are moved to share? Prayer in response to the Word may be a time to name aloud or silently persons near or far away whom the scripture and message brought to mind. An open-ended message may well be followed by silence that is prayerlike, silence to discover what God is saying through this Word to each of us today. (While the playing of music during meditation times is popular in some congregations, true silence has become important in our noisy world.)

A Word that focuses on community might call for a response of singing or saying the Lord's Prayer while joining hands. Or, as a symbol of community and diversity, weave together crepe paper streamers, ribbons, or fabric strips through the gathered assembly into a tightly woven piece that could hang in the worship space.

As you plan worship, consider how the response to the Word might be embodied, not simply verbalized. Let the Word dwell in you richly (Colossians 3:16), involve the gifts within your worshiping community and you will discover many ways in which your congregation may be led to respond to the Word in ways that both fit them and stretch them to be God's people.

Sending Forth: In Mission, with Blessing

In one sense, our worship of the Holy is sufficient unto itself and has no other end than bringing ourselves into God's presence. Yet, scripture shows us that whenever people spend time in God's presence they are sent out to do God's will—Moses is given the Ten Commandments to take back to the Israelites (Exodus 19:16–20:24), Isaiah is sent to God's people (Isaiah 6), the disciples are given the Great Commission (Matthew 28:16-20). So, too, we are sent each week from God's presence out to the world.

While we may be hesitant to leave the Holy Presence, as the disciples were after Jesus was transfigured (Matthew 17:4-8), we go forth renewed, thankful, and with abundant blessings. This may be expressed through a final hymn or song that energizes us to take our worship experience into the world, singing God's praises and committing ourselves to God's work. A litany that expresses our recommitment is also appropriate, as is prayer for our task.

If there is a mission project or trip in the upcoming week, now is the time to commission and ask for blessings for those persons. When persons leave a congregation by moving away, going to college out of town, or going away for military service, having the congregation lay hands on them and then asking a blessing for them can be meaningful for everyone.[10]

Some worshiping groups have a practice of joining hands, either where they are sitting or by making a circle in or around the worship space, and singing a song of commitment to God, each other, and the work of God. Songs often used include: "Blest be the tie that binds," "Bind us together, Lord," "Shalom to you," "We are the body of Christ," and "Make us one."

Often the final blessing is linked with a charge or commission to the gathered worshipers: "Go, in the name of Jesus Christ, in the power of the Holy Spirit to _____," with the task linked to the scripture and message of the day. For example, when the scripture and theme of the day have been the feeding of the five thousand (Luke 9:10-17), a charge might be, "Go, in the name of Jesus Christ, in the power of the Holy Spirit, to see where people are hungering around you, offering physical and spiritual food to meet those needs." Or, for Christmas Eve, "Go, to shine the light of Christ in this world, wherever you are." In addition to the Great Commission in Matthew 28:19-20, some of the epistles include charges/commissions in their endings; see especially 2 Corinthians 13:11-13; Philippians 4:4-7, 4:8-9; Colossians 4:17b; 1 Thessalonians 5:16-18; 1 Timothy 6:11-12; Titus 3:6-8; 2 Peter 2:14-15 and 3:18.

The blessing, also called the benediction, is an important part of the sending, and the most appropriate "final word," as a reminder of God's great mercies as we are leaving the worship experience. The Epistles in the New Testament give us wonderful examples of words for blessings. See especially Romans 16:25a, 27; 1 Corinthians 16:23-24; 2 Corinthians 13:14; Galatians 6:18; Ephesians 6:23-24; Philippians 4:20, 23; 1 Thessalonians 5:23-24; 2 Thessalonians 3:16; 2 Timothy 4:22; Titus 3:4-7; Hebrews 13:20-21; 1 Peter 5:14b; 2 Peter 3:18; 2 John 3; Jude 24-25. Whoever gives the blessing is really a conduit or "realizer" for the blessings that God is constantly giving us, so stand where you may be seen by the congregation and lift your hands in a gracious "calling down of the Spirit." If you regularly give the blessing or even if you only do it once, consider memorizing one of the biblical blessings cited above—your eye contact with the congregation and the blessing these words will bring to your own heart and mind will be of great value.

In many churches there is a tradition of a musical postlude as the final item of the worship service. It has become a tradition in some congregations to use that time as meditation and reflection at the end of the service (and also out of respect for a musician who has prepared this musical reflection). If you want time for meditation or reflection after the message, write it into the service and let it be true silence. If a musical piece can help the whole congregation respond to the Word, write it into the service. The sending forth should be just that, an energizing time of going back into the world; if musical accompaniment is desired, let it be a rousing rendition of the final hymn or another upbeat piece that will let the congregation know that they truly are sent.

Now You're Ready to Plan the Gathering!

Now that you know where the worship experience is headed, it is time to plan for the opening elements that will get you there. This gathering time may include greeting each other and new-comers in the name of God, becoming a community through song, and centering the community through prayer and silence.

Many worshipers find music a helpful vehicle for gathering people together, yet the boundary between "gathering" and "worship" can be very fluid. There is no one "right" way to begin worship, but it does need to be clear to persons that we have moved from being our individual chatty selves into a time together. Here are a variety of ways that congregations have negotiated that time and its boundary; focus on finding one that fits your community so that people will begin to expect to prepare themselves in a particular manner after arriving for worship.

1. If the doors to the worship space open right off the parking lot, or if the reconnection of the community each week is impor-tant, give folks time to check in with each other and chat. Then

at the appointed hour for worship to begin, you have several options:

   a. A worship leader may stand up in front and call the congregation to order with the liturgical reminder, "The Lord/God is with you." To which the congregation responds, "And also with you." Other greetings may be found in worship books or in scripture, including the frequent greeting in the Epistles: "Grace to you and peace from God our Father and the Lord Jesus Christ" (1 Corinthians 1:3; 2 Corinthians 1:2; Ephesians 1:2; Philippians 1:2; 2 Thessalonians 1:2; 1 Timothy 1:2b; 2 Timothy 1:2b; Philemon 3), an expanded version in Galatians 1:3-5 and another in 1 Peter 1:2b-3 and 2 Peter 1:2; or Jude 2's "May mercy, peace, and love be yours in abundance." This method of gathering can lead either to a brief formal prelude and time of individual centering or it may be followed by an opening hymn to draw the community together (either announced for more formal worship, or done as described in #2 for a more informal approach).

   b. As the time approaches, musicians may enter and begin an introduction to a familiar hymn or song that the congregation knows by heart and will join in automatically. Having a common repertoire of "music of the heart" (the combination of strong theology with compelling music, each of which speak to the congregation[11]) makes this a natural way of coming together to worship.

   c. There may be a procession down a center aisle, either by an acolyte to light candles on the altar table or by persons who will draw everyone in with a skit, mime, or other dramatic action. Depending on how ready the gathered community is to settle down, this may be done in silence or may need "processional music."

2. In some worshiping communities, the band or a group of singers gathers well before the appointed time, at least thirty minutes, and then music is already happening when persons begin to enter the worship space. This lends itself to informal singing and occasionally to quiet conversations. The band or singers need to see this time as worship and not performance, as their task is to involve the congregation in singing rather than performing solos.

3. Congregations that are more formal, with the worship space or sanctuary set apart, may prefer silence to prepare them for worship. If this is an important value for the majority of your congregation, then close the doors to the narthex or gathering space, have a musical prelude before the worship time, and an official greeting of the congregation on the hour. If you are an informal congregation, this may not feel like a natural way to begin; if you have been attempting to have silence and it is not happening, then your congregation does not see itself as formal and you need to delineate this time by using one of the other ideas above.

In addition to planning gathering music that enhances and reinforces the scripture and theme planned, consider what sorts of prayers ought to be included in the worship experience. Prayers are available in hymnals and worship books and may be adapted for your setting and service.

1. Many worship services begin by invoking the presence of God, often through the Holy Spirit. This calling on the Spirit, who is already present, declares our intention to be in God's presence and is called an invocation.

2. Some congregations find it helpful to begin by confession of sin and assurance of pardon. This follows the tradition named in Psalm 24 about coming before the Lord with clean hands and pure hearts. Prayers of confession are often best when they include times of silence. It is essential to follow confession with explicit mention of pardon. Passing the peace immediately to each other "as forgiven and reconciled people" enacts this forgiveness in a very holistic way and encourages our forgiveness of those "who have sinned against us" as well as those we have hurt.

3. Some groups use a Call to Worship, which is "call-and-response" and thus involves everyone and usually sets the theme for the day. Many Psalm verses make good Calls to Worship, such as one used traditionally: "This is the day that the Lord has made." **"Let us rejoice and be glad in it"** (Psalm 118:24).

4. More formal or liturgical congregations may include a Collect for the day, which is a short prayer form naming God, petitioning God for a specific gift related to the scripture and day and telling how the congregation will use that gift in the world. Less formal churches may include a congregational or morning prayer or gather "joys and concerns" in this early time in the worship experience. In whatever type of prayer you include, silence and listening to God need to be a part.

Summary

In these two chapters we have discussed the advantages of planning together and some ways to accomplish that if you feel like you are working alone. Begin your planning with a focus on a scripture (or set of scripture readings from the lectionary), the liturgical season or holy day, or a theme. Following a creative process that begins with prayer gives time and shape for gathering ideas and images. Sometimes resources that you select may need adapting for your particular worshiping community; pay attention to their heart language. Then, for each worship experience, consider first how the Word will be proclaimed and heard, then how the congregation may be involved in responding, then how they will be sent back to the world. That process will direct your subsequent planning for the gathering time. Whether you are planning whole services "from scratch" or simply making adaptations to your current service, understanding the movement of worship gives a good foundation. Finally, as you began your worship planning with prayer, give thanks as you end and then plan to gather as worship leaders to pray together again before the actual service begins.

CHAPTER 6

Baptism and Communion

Day by day, as they spent much time together in the temple, they broke bread at home and ate their food with glad and generous hearts. (Acts 2:46)

A Means of Grace

One traditional definition of *sacrament*, the term used by many churches for baptism and communion, is "an outward and visible sign of an inward and spiritual grace." In the New Testament, the word used for *sacrament* is the Greek *mysterion*, which indicates the mystery in which God reveals Godself to us. The word *sacrament* comes from the Latin for *duty* and shares the root word with *sacred*, "to make holy." The sense of duty related to baptism and communion also appears in the denominations that call them *ordinances* because God *ordered* us to participate in them.

While baptism and communion have always been considered *sacraments* or *ordinances* throughout the history of the church, other things were occasionally considered sacraments as well so that by the Middle Ages there were many sacraments. During the Protestant Reformation, Luther defined a sacrament as having three parts: a means of grace (that is God's very self given to us), institution by Jesus Christ, and a physical element (such as water, bread, or wine/juice). Following this understanding, most

71

Protestant churches currently celebrate baptism and communion as the two sacraments.[1]

In this chapter we will briefly discuss the theological and scriptural background for baptism and communion, following each section with some ideas for worship communities from three to ninety-nine to consider. The guidelines for your practices of baptism and communion will be those of your denomination and the principles of hospitality and participation, always seeking to let God's grace flow through you abundantly.

Baptism

"You are my Son, the Beloved; with you I am well pleased."
(Mark 1:11)

Background

Baptism has a place of honor in the Christian faith because Jesus himself was baptized (Matthew 3:13-17, Mark 1:9-11, and Luke 3:21-22). These three accounts all include the use of water, descent of the Holy Spirit in the form of a dove, and God's voice declaring Jesus as Beloved Son. Water played an important role in Hebrew Scriptures: a wind from God swept over the face of the waters (Genesis 1:2), flood in the time of Noah cleansed the earth from sin (Genesis 6–8), the Hebrew people escaped through the Red Sea in the time of Exodus (chapters 14–15) and were given water from a rock (Numbers 20:1-13). Jesus also had important moments around water: calling fishermen to leave their boats and follow him (Mark 1:16-20), teaching by the sea (Mark 4:1-9), talking with a woman sitting by a well (John 4:1-42), and walking on water (John 6:16-21). Water is essential to human life; without it we would die. We are cleansed by it and refreshed by it. On the day of Pentecost, which we understand as the birthday of the church, about three thousand people were baptized and added to the Christian "teaching and fellowship, to the breaking of bread and the prayers" (Acts 2:41-42).

Baptism has been the entryway into Christian fellowship since that time, whether for infants whose parents are church members for new converts of any age. As the early church worked out its understanding of baptism, it came to be multifaceted, beginning with scriptural references in addition to those above.

❑ Salvation—1 Peter 3:21
❑ New birth—John 3:5
❑ Water and the Spirit—Acts 11:15-16
❑ Renouncing spiritual forces of wickedness—Ephesians 6:11-12
❑ Forgiveness and cleansing from sin—Hebrews 10:22
❑ Clothing us in Christ—Galatians 3:27
❑ Dying and being raised with Christ—Romans 6:3-5, Colossians 2:12, 3:1, Ephesians 2:5-6
❑ Becoming children of light—Ephesians 5:14

Other facets of baptism evolved in the theology of the church:

❑ As a New Covenant—just as the Jews were circumcised to represent the covenant between God and Abraham, so Christians were baptized to represent the covenant between God and humanity through Jesus Christ (and this covenant was opened to both genders).
❑ Belief in the Trinity—seen in the development of the Apostles' Creed, used historically as three questions: Do you believe in God the Father? Do you believe in Jesus Christ? Do you believe in the Holy Spirit?
❑ Following the way of Jesus Christ, liberation, the beginning of our spiritual journey, and our commitment to Christ

The Sacrament of Baptism in Congregations from Three to Ninety-nine

Many congregations or worshiping groups could benefit from a study of baptism, using the service itself as a starting point, the biblical references noted above, or the baptismal hymns in your hymnal. The season of Lent was historically a season of preparation for baptism at Easter, so it is an appropriate time for this study; but ordinary time could work also, perhaps beginning with the Sunday after January 6, that celebrates the baptism of Jesus and going through the Season after the Epiphany up to Ash Wednesday and the beginning of Lent.

Whatever your tradition of baptizing, make certain that water is an abundant symbol and towels are available. In many places, sponsors take the place of what used to be understood as godparents, that is, persons who guide the baptized on their spiritual journey; these persons can have a role in the actual ritual, pouring the water or reading a scripture. In a worshiping community that is the right size to gather around the font or pool, invite everyone into that space at the beginning of the baptismal ritual, and then include all in the laying on of hands after the water has been applied. Some worshiping communities include a song or hymn about baptism that has become a tradition for them at each baptism or the lighting of a baptismal candle. Baptismal candles are long pillar candles, lit within the service, and sent home with the baptized person, to be lit on the anniversary of their baptism or on their birthday to remind that this person is a child of God. Baptism was historically followed by the candidate's first communion, so keep the sermon short this day and let the sacraments speak the Word.

Other ideas for baptismal services for congregations up to one hundred will be found in the sections on baptism in chapter 3. Services of reaffirmation of baptism are also becoming more popular as persons seek to keep the energy and blessing of their baptismal day in front of them. Reaffirmation may be done yearly, each time someone in the congregation is baptized, or even by simply having the font available for persons to touch the water as they enter the worship space or go up to receive communion.

Holy Communion

When [Jesus] was at the table with them, he took bread, blessed and broke it, and gave it to them. Then their eyes were opened, and they recognized him (Luke 24:30-31a).

Background

Although Protestant churches traditionally take their foundation for communion from Paul's understanding of it in 1 Corinthians 11:23-25 and the Gospel stories telling of the Last Supper (Matthew 26:26-30; Mark 14:22-25; Luke 22:14-20), those congregations that are seeking to meet God at the communion table as a joyful and empowering action will do well to consider the walk-to-Emmaus story and the lines quoted above, for communion is not simply the remembrance of Jesus' last meal with his disciples—that final meal had a wealth of memories for them: "Taste and see that the LORD is good" (Psalm 34:8); mention of daily bread in the prayer that Jesus gave them (Matthew 6:11, Luke 11:3); Jesus feeding the multitude (Mark 6:30-44), four thousand (Mark 8:1-10), and five thousand (Matthew 14:13-21, Luke 9:10-17, John 6:1-15); Jesus eating with sinners (Matthew 11:18-19; Mark 2:18-20; Luke 5:33-35, 7:33-35, and 15:1-2), with friends and challengers (Mark 14:1-9; Luke 10:38-42; 14:1-6, and 24:13-35; John 2:1-11, 12:1-8, and 21:9-14); stories Jesus told them about banquets, baking, rich, poor (Matthew 22:1-10; Luke 13:20-21, 14:7-14, 14:15-24, and 16:19-31); Jesus' announcement that he was the bread of life (John 6:25-59).

The early church made communion—called *Eucharist*, from the Greek, to remind them that it was primarily *thanksgiving* to God—a regular part of their worship experiences and their life together (Acts 2:42-46). Over time, they began to develop theological interpretations of it: we become one body during communion (1 Corinthians 10:16-18), how the body of Christ is to be (1 Corinthians 12:4-26), the power of the meal to help us grow up in salvation (1 Peter 2:2-3). These were colored by the vision of John and the marriage supper that will happen at the end of time (Revelation 7:16 and 19:9).

Over the centuries the balance between the holiness and uniqueness of the meal and its reminder to us of the food we need for our spiritual journey every day has been in flux. During the Middle Ages, communion was considered so holy that persons only partook of the bread once a year. As a result of Vatican II, the Liturgical Renewal movement, and the emphasis in worship on the whole person, communion is currently becoming more frequent in many worship experiences, and we are invited to take an "abundant foretaste" of the bread and cup. Throughout the ages there has been a basic fourfold pattern of the *taking* of the elements by the presider from the people, of *blessing* the elements, *breaking* the bread, and *giving* the elements to the assembled congregation.

The Sacrament of Communion in Congregations from Three to Ninety-nine

Since communion involves all of our senses (smell and taste of bread and wine/juice, touch of the cup on lips and bread in hands, sounds of prayer, visual and kinesthetic sense of joining with others to receive), many congregations are including it in their worship more frequently. In chapter 3, on worship space, we discussed various ways of receiving communion in different worship spaces. Like baptism, a communion study can deepen the worshiping community's understanding and participation in this sacrament.

Some congregations find it meaningful to gather, after passing the peace, around the altar table for the Great Thanksgiving, or communion prayer, and the receiving. These congregations plan their worship space to include sufficient room around the table for this to happen. When gathering persons around the table, use familiar spoken or sung responses so that people will have their hands free.[2] Other congregations may stay in their seats for the prayer and come forward for receiving either by "tables," that is, however many can easily circle the table at one time, or in a steady stream of persons.[3]

Some worshiping congregations find it helpful and formational to use one basic communion prayer with congregational responses that are unchanging while the leader's words change slightly, according to scripture, theme, or liturgical season. Others will seek more variation in the prayers, using worship books and resources for the appropriate words and responses. For some, sung responses will be the easiest to remember; there are many options available in hymnals and worship resources.

Involving the congregation in communion may take the shape of preparing the table and the elements (including baking bread), holding the book for the presider, participating in responses (everyone, not just a choir), serving each other, cleaning up after communion, or taking communion to those unable to attend that day's service. For expansion on these and other ideas, see my *Communion Services*.

Quoting from *Communion Services* for serving each other in a circle:

> During the distribution, each person breaks off the bread for the person on their right, gives it to them saying appropriate words, and passes the bread to the left. The chalice follows behind, with the person on the left holding the chalice for the person on their right, saying appropriate words to them, as the person on the right dips bread in the chalice. Then the chalice is also passed to the left. Although this may sound complicated, it can be easily learned, as the pattern is simply "serve right, pass left." The complexity comes in how the first persons handle the bread and chalice; it is probably best if the pastor or presider helps things to get started correctly and then receives Communion last. Because everyone will speak during this distribution, singing would be distracting during this time, especially in a small group.[4]

One other idea for congregations of three to ninety-nine would be to include communion as part of a potluck or prepared meal. This follows early Christian tradition, hinted at in 1 Corinthians 11:17-22 and 27-33, often misinterpreted to keep persons away from the table. Paul is writing to criticize the greediness of some Corinthians (the nonworking) of arriving at the meal that included communion and eating all the good food before others (the working folks) arrive. So "when you come together to eat, wait for one another" (1 Corinthians 11:33), and surround this full meal with the holy meal by beginning with communion and suggesting some "holy conversation starters" so that the time might include talk about people's faith journeys and thanksgivings.

Summary

The sacraments are a means of grace, which means that through them we may experience God's abundant love and mercy in our lives. The intimate relationship that worship communities of three to ninety-nine provide naturally affords the opportunity for increased participation in each of the sacraments, as we gather around the baptismal font and around the communion table. The sacraments provide important opportunities for worship to be biblical and traditional, communal and contemporary, missional, holistic, participatory, formational, and authentic, as we stand or kneel before the Triune Grace in need of grace and sure to receive.

CHAPTER 7

The Arts in Worship

Sing to the LORD a new song. (Psalm 96:1)

Art is part of the essential context for our worship, whether consciously or unconsciously—the place where we meet; lighting, whether natural or artificial; physical materials of wood, concrete, glass, aluminum, stone, plastic, silk, cotton, felt, wool, linen, ceramics, metal, in the meeting space, in vessels used for communion and to hold baptismal water, at the windows, on tables or chairs; sounds of silence, music, or traffic; smells of bread, incense, or flowers; colors throughout; smooth or rough surfaces; taste of bread and wine/juice; movement and stillness through the space. Using our space and marking it as holy are an important part of the preparation for worship as well as during it.

In chapter 2, we discussed the varieties of gifts that can be used to enhance the worship space, and in chapter 3, we discussed how space affects worship. There was brief mention of color and its softening effects, by draping fabric, to warm up a worship space. One simple example of the use of color to enhance the worship space may be seen at Taizé (found online at www.taize.fr/en_rubrique12.html), where the use of orange and yellow cloth to represent the Holy Spirit gives a light-filled focus to the worship space. Using colors of the liturgical season or colors related to a theme (blue and sea green for baptism, wheat and grape colors for communion, deep purple for the Reign of Christ Sunday) can warm up and focus any space quickly.

Be certain that lighting both makes it possible for people to participate and fits the mood of the service. It is easy in our hope to create a peaceful, meditative service to dim the lights so much that hymns and prayers cannot be read by congregation or leaders. (Beware of this with Christmas Eve candle-lighting and perhaps plan to sing the final stanza of "Silent Night" without accompaniment.) At times you may be able to darken one part of the room to give the illusion of dark and calm while keeping the other part lit enough for reading. Conversely, if you are using media projection in a room with a lot of natural light, you will need to provide drapes or other window covering as needed for the projection to be visible.

In most groups of three to ninety-nine, hearing one another is not the concern that it might be in larger groups and larger buildings. Make it possible for persons to gather closely enough to hear one another (that also improves the singing!) and remind all leaders to speak clearly and distinctly. Be certain that sight lines are clear for all to see the speaker because that assists in our hearing. If you are using instruments to accompany singing, they should support rather than overpower the singers—more on that below.

Whether you are using bulletins or projecting slides, be sure to use a reasonable type size for reading. And in either instance do not use all caps, which signifies shouting, for the congregational part—use bold or a larger font; it will be easier for folks to read. Sense lines, breaking where we would pause for breath, for meaning, or for extended congregational reading are also helpful; for example, it is easier for people to read:

> Our Father who art in heaven,
>   hallowed be thy name.
> Thy kingdom come,
>   thy will be done on earth as it is in heaven.

than it is to read "Our Father who art in heaven, hallowed be thy name. Thy kingdom come, thy will be done on earth as it is in heaven." Using sense lines will also force you to consider the length and wordiness of your prayers. Projecting songs requires using sense lines also; type the song or hymn text as you would type a poem. Beware of overusing graphics and background designs on bulletins and projection that blurs or makes any text difficult to read.

Music of the Heart

"Music of the heart" is a term used to describe John and Charles Wesley's use of strong theological texts with compelling music to assist worshiping groups to participate, be shaped in faith, and remember to whom they belong and how they are called to live.[1] It's hard for some to imagine Christmas without "Hark the herald angels sing" or Easter without "Christ the Lord is risen today," both Charles Wesley hymns. Compelling music and strong theological texts are good criteria to keep in mind when selecting music for worship today. Music is one of the most debated aspects of worship and has been for centuries. It has the power to energize and to soothe but also to seduce us into singing bad theology and tacky music; make sure that what you select to sing not only speaks to the moment but also has the integrity to take the congregation into the future.

Referring back to chapter 1, other criteria for the use of music in worship are:

❑ Trinitarian—Does our music sing about all three persons of the Trinity and about the one God? Is God both near and far, both companion and creator?

❑ Biblical—Are the texts scriptural or at least true to the arc of scripture? If not, don't sing them!

❑ Traditional—Have we included some texts and tunes that have spoken to Christians throughout the ages and are part of our heritage as Christians?

❑ Sacramental—Is our singing filled with grace? Is it coaxed from the congregation rather than forced out of them? Do we have songs that hold meaning for times of baptism and communion?

❏ Communal—Worship may be the only place persons sing regularly besides birthdays. Yet, we are called to "sing to the Lord," and music has the ability to draw us together as community to praise and to lament, to pray and to receive the Spirit. There are a number of simple ways to encourage congregational singing and expand your worship music repertoire (see appendix 2, license sites). Don't let music be taken away from the worshiping congregation—instruments, choirs, and praise bands are there not to entertain but to assist the congregation in finding its voice to praise God.

❏ Contemporary—Are you learning a "new song" (Psalm 96:1)? Do you have music that speaks to different generations, to young and old? Are you giving space for all voices in the congregation to have a turn in leading with their voice and then supporting others? Music is a buffet, not a one-note supper!

❏ Missional—Does your singing remind you of the world around you each week? Does it represent different countries and cultures? Does it energize your congregation for mission?

❏ Holistic—Many congregations are finding that clapping and swaying are not out of place in worship, but indeed help them to bring their whole selves to God in worship. Is there room in your music and your worship for that? How might you let that happen?

❏ Participatory—Does everyone in the worshiping community feel encouraged to sing and feel that their voice is sufficient? This last may take some work from the leadership to help people find their voice, to "make a joyful noise" (Psalm 100:1), to join together to praise God.[2] Persons who truly love to sing, who find themselves singing in the car, at work, in the Sunday school hall, are the persons who can help the congregation "get there."

❏ Formational—Are we using texts and tunes that form us into the kind of people God calls us to be? Do our songs build up? Does the way we introduce them and repeat them encourage people to grow in faith and give them words for telling the Good News?

❑ Authentic—Finally, are the songs and hymns we are singing authentic both to who we are now and to who we are called to be? Will we be able to join the song of the angels at the end of time and also add a new song? Does our singing relate to the best of our life outside worship and express our true feelings? This means lament as well as praise, sadness as well as joy, confession as well as petition.

The best musicians for worship are those who understand not only the art of music but also how worship works and how to make singing together a compelling and grace-filled experience for everyone in the congregation. So choose leaders with heart and soul, who have good eye contact, who breathe, who can show pitches (up and down) with their hands rather than a beat pattern (one, two, three, and so on). Look to your local seminary or Christian college if you need some encouragement and direction, but letting your own folks do the leading will be the best. The vitality of a worshiping congregation may often be seen in how they sing together—let yours shine!

Touch and Taste of Communion

The art of bread-baking may enhance your communion service. Pay attention to any allergies present in the congregation. Stay with "ordinary" breads that break well and taste good. Baking the bread near the worship space, or warming it up, can add the sense of smell to that of taste; Sunday school that meets before worship can be an ideal time to work on this. Likewise, choose a good-tasting grape juice or wine for communion. The vessels should be clean and appropriate to the scale of your worship space, as should any linen you might use. Some congregations worry about spending more money than they have on the vessels for communion, and while there is something to be said for sacrificial giving and the beauty of the worship space, simple things done well are very appropriate. And if you have potters, silversmiths, glassblowers, or seamstresses among you, find examples of vessels and communion linens for them to use as guides for making things to use.

For worship experiences that include communion, keep the altar table free of other things. This is a day to put flowers, offering plates, and any other decorations on a side table. Let communion vessels, bread and cup, and the book for prayer have the center place on the table and in the celebration.

Learning to serve each other is a wonderful gift to Christian community and it affects our sense of touch. Graciousness is the first principle and hospitality close to it. Build one another up as you learn to serve one another; see the section on Communion in chapter 6 for some ideas about serving one another. Break off sufficient pieces of bread in order to keep fingers out of the cup into which you are dipping. If you are using individual glasses, in the service, thank those who have prepared and will clean them. Out of respect for the environment, do not use disposable cups or plates, please! If you are communing around tables, even children can help to set them for communion.

Passing the peace, a tradition inherited from the early church, can be a meaningful part of communion or any service. In communion, it is particularly related to the relationships between human beings, that is, reconciliation. It generally follows the prayer of confession before the Great Thanksgiving. Persons should move out of their seats or pews to greet one another in the name of Jesus Christ and offer peace ("The peace of Christ be with you." **"And also with you."** Or, "God's peace"). This greeting is to be extended to those we know and those we don't know, those we like and those we don't like. It is a time to practice Christian hospitality and reconciliation, knowing that we can share God's love even if we don't feel that yet. Passing the peace may be a handshake or hug, or simply eye contact. Watch for clues and honor anyone's request (verbal or unspoken) not to be touched, no matter what their age—that's simply part of the respect they are to be given as a child of God.

Touch and Sound of Baptismal Waters

The sound of water pouring from a pitcher into a font, a running fountain, even a rainstick, can enhance our hearing and appreciation of God's use of water in baptism. Let water be abundant and have thick, comfortable toweling available for candidates, who will indeed get wet. It is possible to have persons in your congregation make the pitcher and font, and there are less expensive options to some of the expensive sets in catalogs. There is nothing unholy about finding your bowl and pitcher in a good kitchen supply store; just make sure it is plain, without decoration other than the color of the material. Pick vessels that fit the scale of your worship space; glass or pottery are most often used today. Having time for everyone to "remember that they are baptized" and come to touch the water after the candidates have been baptized can also be meaningful.

Baptism provides a particularly meaningful opportunity for congregations of three to ninety-nine to gather around the one being baptized and to "lay on hands." Laying on hands has been passed down since biblical times as a way of signifying blessing and the power of the Holy Spirit. It may be done during baptism, confirmation, ordination, or for healing. It is absolutely essential that all touch in worship be safe and appropriate. So laying on of hands occurs around the head or top of the shoulders and may also occur by placing one's hands above the head. Touching hands themselves may also be appropriate. If only one person lays on hands it would be done on the head, but if the congregation is invited to all participate, then each person would appropriately touch the person nearest them on the hand or shoulder. This can be a powerful action for the recipient and for all involved when it is God's power flowing through. But also honor anyone's request to not be touched, no matter what their age might be— that's simply part of the respect they are to be given as a child of God (just as in passing the peace).

Creating or Commissioning Art for Your Worship

Some worshiping congregations will want to create some of the art used in worship themselves and others may wish to commission a liturgical artist to do so. The art might include a stained-glass window, communion or baptismal vessels, a special altar table or hanging cross, a symbol of Easter, a drama for a home-coming, a banner, a video of your mission trip to share in worship, or a song for the anniversary of your congregation.

Whether you ask someone in the congregation or a liturgical artist to create something for you, the process is fairly similar. Find someone whose work you have observed in the medium that you are seeking, or ask persons from other congregations. Plan on paying for supplies for someone in the congregation or a liturgical artist; plan on paying additional monies to a liturgical artist for their time because that's how they make their living. Expect questions about how the art will function in worship and about the congregation—it needs to fit your congregation in order to express your worship of God. What may seem insignificant to you about belief or circumstance may be exactly the question that sparks a liturgical artist's idea for the art for your worship to God. The scale of your worship space, needs for transportability, your budget, and your time limits will all affect how gracefully the commission proceeds. Working with persons from your congrega-tion will have the same issues, perhaps more subtly, perhaps not; whatever you do, let everyone's behavior be Christian.

Summary

Our worship is shaped by our spaces and by what we put in them—color, light, communion and baptismal vessels and linens, music, sounds of pouring water, the smell of bread. Go back to chapter 2 and consider the various gifts your worshiping commu-nity has to share. How can they find an outlet that will make your worship more hospitable, participatory, and authentic? What does your worship space reflect of God's great beauty in nature and through human use of the arts? This chapter included ideas for color, light, music, baptism, communion, and creating and commissioning such work that in all things God may be glorified.

CHAPTER 8

Select Ideas for Congregations up to One Hundred

For everything there is a season, and a time for every matter under heaven. (Ecclesiastes 3:1)

The Christian Year in Practice

During the **Incarnation Cycle,** take time to prepare spiritually for Christmas and then to dwell into Incarnation during the twelve days from Christmas to Epiphany. Don't be afraid to be an alternative to the consumer-driven nature of North American Christmas. Teach children and the rest of your worshiping community some of the religious carols that are no longer being taught in schools. Take care to adapt any Christmas programs or cantatas to your own situation, and recognize that the best words for the season are those from scripture.[1] Your worshiping community can have some wonderful time together studying and creating things related to symbols of Christ's coming. Make this a time of mission outreach to those who really need our gifts. Remember the gift of candlelight in the wintry times of the Northern Hemisphere, something that draws in persons of every age.

The **Paschal Cycle,** Lent-Easter-Pentecost, was originally a time for preparation for baptism and for reconnecting to the church. Use images and the many facets of baptism and discipleship to guide your worship planning. Holy Week, with its procession of Palms, Last Supper remembrance, and walking with Jesus to the cross, can be very meaningful with groups that are the right size to get everyone involved. Consider an Easter vigil or Easter Eve service, which includes readings from the Bible about God's gift of salvation, lighting the Paschal Candle and individual candles, baptism, and communion. During the Great Fifty Days, celebrate the presence of the risen Christ with communion every week. If you include outreach to the broader community by hosting an Easter egg hunt, be certain to include the resurrection story and an Easter song or two during the gathering, before everyone scatters to find the goodies.

Ordinary time can be broken down into month-long foci on a book of the Bible or theological topic or something new in worship. Make sure to rotate your worship teams so that no one gets too tired to keep their faith and creativity flowing in these times. If you are in an area that relaxes more during this season, relax worship a bit by holding it outdoors; include more singing or praying and more involvement from everyone. Persons who are busier during the school year may have more time to help with worship planning and arts during the summer; plan ahead to involve them.

Worship and Pastoral Rites

Confirmation: As part of confirmation, have the confirmands, with assistance perhaps from a liturgical artist, create a banner representing the congregation and their own place in it; bring these out in future confirmations to celebrate the continuing heritage of faith. Include sponsors, mentors, or parents in laying on hands as persons are confirmed. Train confirmands to serve communion at this service at stations around the sanctuary, including serving their own families.

For **Services of Christian Marriage & Covenant:** Keep God front and center in your planning so that the service will be a worship experience; congregational singing and prayers may enhance the service. To celebrate the marriage of persons from the congregation, gather a group to create a special altar table-cloth or banner that will be used for that wedding and henceforth in the church. Take a cue from the 1994 movie version of "Little Women" and surround the bride and groom singing, perhaps, "For the beauty of the earth" as the film did or your congregational song of blessing directed to these two and their union. Another place where more intimate congregations can be help-ful in life-passage events is to think creatively about costs, in order that weddings do not place undue burdens on people— what about using skills found within the congregation for the service and the reception?

For **Services of Death & Resurrection:** Consider concluding the service with the congregational blessing song. Creating a funeral pall that belongs to the congregation is a good way to honor those who die and remind us all of the connection between our baptism and our death—both take place in Christ and assure us of salvation. Find a good linen or satin cloth to hem and include a central symbol from baptism. Another place where more intimate congregations can be helpful in life-passage events is to think creatively about costs, so that funerals do not place undue burdens on people—meal preparation is often an impor-tant part of death rituals in close-knit communities; a community pall means that the casket does not need to be exceptionally ornate and expensive.

Prayer Services, Including Those for Healing

Groups of three to forty-nine are conducive to the kind of inti-mate sharing that can happen in prayer services, including those for healing. Because we have described worship as holistic, asking for prayer for healing—physical, mental, emotional, spiritual—is very appropriate in ordinary worship experiences, while monthly or quarterly services might focus on prayer. Introduce this type of service with the many scripture passages where Jesus healed persons; this may also be part of a parish-nurse or church-hospital connection in your overall ministries. One good way to ease people's way toward attending is to remind them that praying for others is as important as praying for our own personal healing—we pray for others we love and for those we don't know, maybe the parent of a co-worker, or someone we read about in the news, or an area of the world that is in turmoil. Careful planning, attention to a person's reactions to prayer and occasional follow-up are all part of the pastoral care that surrounds this type of service. Gather a team of at least three persons to plan and to pray for each person who comes forward with a request for themselves or someone else—rotate praying and laying on of hands, and offer anointing of hand or forehead.[2] This service typically has a shorter gathering time; focus on one of the biblical healing stories or other scriptures such as James 5:14-16a; Isaiah 40:28-31; Psalms 27, 41, or 91; or Romans 8. You may have a short message and then plan plenty of time for prayer, silent and spoken, individually and with groups, followed by a strong and calm sending forth.

Larger Celebratory Gatherings

These can be a good change from your own congregation each week and may include:

1. Homecomings, where persons related more loosely to your congregation or who have moved away, come back to worship followed by a potluck dinner.

2. Ecumenical gatherings large or small, for example:

a. Celebrating Thanksgiving and Ash Wednesday with another church, alternating whose space you meet in with who brings the message
b. Gathering with other churches in your geographic area for a yearly choir festival or worship experience
c. Gathering with other churches in your denomination for confirmation or Pentecost

3. Parishes on a circuit (several congregations that share a pastor) may gather for Christmas Sunday or Pentecost, or fifth Sunday hymn-sings and potlucks.

4. If your group is part of a larger congregation (daughter/mother or satellite churches), gather together for worship on a regular basis, to celebrate a holy day or mission, or to celebrate the church's anniversary.

Summary

Through the liturgical year and life-related rituals, keep your eyes, minds, and hearts open for the ways in which you might involve persons' gifts for worship and the advantages of your size of congregation. Prayer services and combined events with other congregations and denominations can also bring blessings.

Afterword

The grace of the Lord Jesus Christ be with your spirit.
(Philippians 4:23)

In the first chapter, we described worship as an encounter with the experience of God as Trinity, as biblical and traditional, sacramental, communal and contemporary, missional, holistic, participatory, formational, and authentic. The distinctive character of worship in gatherings of up to one hundred persons begins with the foundational understanding that this gathering is the right size, "wherever two or three are gathered." This worship builds on shared experience where every person can add her or his gift to worship leadership. Worship with groups of this size is a workshop for Christian life together.

I hope you have found some helpful ideas and some inspiration in these pages. Christian worship is vital to our life together and for strengthening our faith and Christian living. We neglect it at our peril. Yet, when we give it the prayerful time and attention that it deserves, we create vital communities that are hospitable and grace-filled, that worship with their whole beings—heart and mind and soul and strength—and that go forth to the world filled with God's spirit. May it be so for you!

Discerning Our Gifts

Interest Survey

I am interested in or have skills in the following areas (check all that apply):

I have seen these skills and interests in _____ (name other persons):

_____Artistic

_____Baking bread

_____Candle-making

_____Clear speaking voice

_____Communication

_____Computer/typing

_____Construction/building

_____Courage to talk with strangers

_____Creative

_____Detail management

_____Development of faith

_____Discernment

_____Drama

_____Dramatic reading

_____Energetic

_____Engaging presence

_____Flexibility

_____Flower arranging

_____Follow-through

_____Gardening

_____Giving money
_____Good eye contact
_____Good listening skills
_____Graciousness
_____Hospitality
_____Housekeeping
_____Including others
_____Listening to music
_____Looking at art
_____Love of prayer
_____Love of scripture
_____Love of study
_____Love of words
_____Making video/filming
_____Muscle
_____Openness to new ideas
_____Organization
_____Oversight
_____Painting
_____Passing on the faith and its traditions
_____People-persons
_____Photography
_____Planning
_____Playing musical instruments (list which ones)
_____Possibility thinker
_____PowerPoint
_____Prayer life
_____Public speaking
_____Publicity
_____Research and analysis skills
_____Sensitivity to others' comfort levels
_____Sewing or working with fabric
_____Singing
_____Speak other languages
_____Steady sense of rhythm
_____Storytelling
_____Team player
_____Welcoming
_____Willingness to encourage others
_____Willingness to share faith

_____Willingness to speak to someone new
_____Woodworking
_____Working with clay or metal
_____Working with toddlers
_____Working with children
_____Working with youth
_____Working with others
_____Writing

Resources: A Sample Basic Worship Library

Print Materials

Bush, Peter, and Christine O'Reilly. *Where 20 or 30 Are Gathered: Leading Worship in the Small Church. Vital Worship, Healthy Congregations Series.* Herndon, Va.: The Alban Institute, 2006.

Harrelson, Walter J., ed. *The New Interpreter's Study Bible.* Nashville: Abingdon Press, 2003.

Klein, Patricia S. *Worship Without Words: The Signs and Symbols of Our Faith.* Brewster, Mass.: Paraclete Press, 2000, 2006.

Knowles Wallace, Robin. *Things They Never Tell You Before You Say "Yes": The Nonmusical Tasks of the Church Musician.* Nashville: Abingdon Press, 1994.

Weaver, Jann Cather, Roger William Wedell, and Kenneth T. Lawrence. *Imaging the Word: An Arts and Lectionary Resource.* 3 vols. Cleveland: Pilgrim Press, 1994.

Your denominational hymnal or a standard hymnal and its companion, such as:

Young, Carlton R., ed. *The United Methodist Hymnal.* Nashville: The United Methodist Publishing House, 1989.

Young, Carlton R. *Companion to The United Methodist Hymnal.* Nashville: Abingdon Press, 1993.

One or more of the following:

Book of Common Prayer (Episcopalian). New York: Church Publishing Incorporated, 1979.

Book of Common Worship (Presbyterian). Louisville: Westminster John Knox, 1993.

Chalice Worship (Disciples of Christ/Christian Church). Edited by Colbert S. Cartwright and O. I. Cricket Harrison. St. Louis: Chalice Press, 1997.

Just in Time! Series. Nashville: Abingdon Press.

    Carter, Kenneth H., Jr. *Baptism Services, Sermons, and Prayers,* 2006.

    ————. *Easter Services, Sermons, and Prayers,* 2007.

    Danals, Cynthia L. *Funeral Services,* 2007.

    Joyner, F. Belton, Jr. *Pastoral Prayers in Public Places,* 2006.

    Knowles Wallace, Robin. *Communion Services,* 2006.

    ————. *Palm Sunday and Holy Week Services,* 2006.

    Mosser, David N. *Stewardship Services,* 2007.

    Phillips, Sara Webb. *Pastoral Prayers for the Hospital Visit,* 2006.

    Rogne, David G. *Advent Services,* 2007.

New Zealand Prayer Book (The Anglican Church of Aotearoa, New Zealand and Polynesia). San Francisco: HarperSanFrancisco, 1997.

Songs and Prayers from Taizé (Community of Taizé). Chicago: GIA Publications, 1991.

The United Methodist Book of Worship. Nashville: The United Methodist Publishing House, 1992.

Wee Worship (Iona Community). Glasgow, Scotland: Wild Goose Publications, 1999.

Online Resources

Bible Sites

http://bible.oremus.org—Bible site that includes the NRSV translation
www.biblegateway.com—Bible site with a variety of search possibilities

Worship Music Sites

www.cyberhymnal.org—The Cyber Hymnal, for texts, tunes (also played), authors, composers
www.hymnsite.com—Includes all of the public domain material from *The United Methodist Hymnal*, 1989
www.printandpraise.com—Print and Praise, a subscription service to download and print worship music from a variety of publishers, including OCP, GIA, and Hope

License Sites

www.ccli.com—Christian Copyright Licensing International, the largest selection of praise and worship music and publishers
www.licensingonline.org—LicenSing, includes mainline publishers
www.onelicense.net—OneLicense, includes mainline publishers and GIA, which holds licenses for Taizé and Iona music

"Music of the Heart": Expanding Your Worship Music Repertoire

Begin by gathering a group of people at church or home who are interested in singing or who are part of an established group (Bible study, prayer time, women's or men's group, youth group, children's Sunday school class, administrative council). If the congregation numbers up to fifty, you might do this as part of a potluck supper or over several informal gathering times in worship. Ask each person present to name a favorite hymn and tell why it's a favorite. If there is time, sing the first stanza of each hymn as it is named, either making a list or marking a hymnal ("Jane's favorite"). If you do this process of singing familiar things without relying on accompaniment, you will begin to build the congregation's ability to sing. This is the beginning of uncovering your congregation's repertoire of "music of the heart."

Then have a musician or worship leader sit down with the list or hymnal and go through it, noting the tune that accompanies each favorite. Each tune has a name, generally listed on the hymn's page in ALL CAPS or CAPS AND SMALL CAPS. While texts are very important for teaching theology and expressing our faith, it is the tune that determines for most people whether or not the hymn is "singable." On the hymn page, along with the tune name, you will also find its meter, either a series of numbers (such as 86.86) or letters (CM, SM, Irr., and so on). The meter is the number of syllables that each line of the hymn, both text and tune, contains; you can also discover the meter yourself by counting the syllables in each line of the text. Some meters are used frequently enough to be named:

CM=Common Meter=86.86

SM=Short Meter=66.86

LM=Long Meter=88.88

D=double, meaning that the meter pattern occurs twice in each stanza; for example, CMD=86.86 times two, or 86.86.86.86 for each stanza or verse

Irr.=Irregular, generally meters that are so unusual that there is only one match for each text/tune

Write down the tune name and its meter. Most likely there will be a variety of meters represented and some meters with multiple tunes. For example, under CM, you may have AZMON, a tune for "O for a Thousand Tongues to Sing" and AMAZING GRACE (also called NEW BRITAIN). Since they share a meter, that means that the words to "Amazing Grace" can be sung to AZMON and vice versa. Try it and see how the texts and tunes fit together, and also how a different tune gives the text a different feel.

The doubling of some texts or tunes adds other interesting possibilities. When the tune is doubled, with eight lines, you can sing two verses of a four-line text to it. When the text is eight lines, you will need to sing a four-line tune twice to fit the text. When there are an odd number of verses, you will need to use half of the tune or repeat a stanza to make things come out even.

You have just discovered the key that can multiply your worship music repertoire exponentially!

❑ Trade known texts and tunes within the same meter to add freshness to the text.

❑ As variation use doubled tunes with texts.

❑ Use a text without refrain to the tune of the same meter that has a refrain. An example of this would be singing the text of either "Amazing Grace" or "O for a Thousand Tongues to

Sing" to the tune of the verse of O How I Love Jesus (CM with refrain) and then singing the refrain "O How I Love Jesus."

❏ Sing new texts to familiar tunes instead of unknown tunes, thus encouraging more confident singing from the congregation. Printing the text as poetry, rather than interlined between music staves, assists this process; consider using public domain texts or purchase a copyright license for your congregation (see appendix 2, license sites).

❏ Learn a new tune that has a meter that can be used for multiple texts and then sing the tune frequently until it becomes part of the repertoire of the congregation.

❏ As you switch texts and tunes, pay attention to the mood of the tune so that the text matches appropriately.

Remember that many early congregations (in Acts and then on the frontiers of North America) did not have keyboards to accompany them or even hymnbooks to sing from. Using "music of the heart" and drawing on familiar tunes can enliven our singing and strengthen our worship.

Glossary

Acolyte: Person who lights the candles on the altar table using a candle lighter or acolyte stick; may also assist pastor with duties during the worship service.

Advent: Season that prepares us for the coming of Christ, first in the Incarnation, second at the end of time. Begins on fourth Sunday before Christmas. In earlier times primarily seen as penitential and shared color purple with Lent; in recent times in North America, blue used as a color of hope and expectation.

Advent wreath: Usually an evergreen wreath with four purple or blue candles (occasionally three purple/blue candles and one pink), which are lit each Sunday in Advent to mark the coming of the Christ.

Altar guild: Persons who gather to prepare worship space: bringing flowers, checking candlewicks, setting out paraments or communion elements, putting water in baptismal font or pitcher.

Altar table: The communion table, reminding that Christ was sacrificed once for all; where we gather in the sacrament of communion to remember his life and work for us.

Ascension: Thursday forty days after Easter, when Christ physically ascended into heaven (Luke 24:50-53, Acts 2:32-33); varies with date of Easter; during the Great Fifty Days. Worship may be held on Ascension Day itself or the Sunday before.

Ash Wednesday: Wednesday that marks the beginning of Lent, with marking of ashes to remember mortality (often using Psalm 51). Worship may be held in morning, at noon, or in evening. Varies with date of Easter.

Baptism: Sacrament of initiation into the body of Christ, by water and the Spirit. According to various traditions candidates for baptism may be any age; always takes place within a worshiping community.

Benediction: Final blessing said at close of worship (literally, good word).

Candidate (for baptism): Person being baptized.

Chalice: Cup used in communion to hold wine or juice.

Chancel: Area of sanctuary with pulpit and altar table; may also contain baptismal font and choir.

Christ candle: Large candle lit on Christmas and the 12 days through Epiphany, signifies God's coming to the world in Jesus Christ; placed in the middle of Advent wreath or separately on altar table.

Christmas: December 25, celebrating Jesus Christ's birth and God's incarnation into human history (Luke 2 and John 1). Worship may be held on Christmas Day or Christmas Eve. Preceded by season of Advent, followed by twelve days of Christmas, ending in Epiphany.

Clergy: Persons who are ordained—such as pastors, priests, or presiders; as opposed to *laity*, the rest of the congregation. Some denominations have persons who are not ordained but are licensed or commissioned to preside at baptism and communion; these persons function as clergy.

Communion, or Holy Communion (see also Eucharist and Lord's Supper) Celebration of Christ's presence with us through bread and wine/juice, which represents his body and his blood; name recalls communing with God and with one another.

Communion elements: Bread, representing the body of Christ, and wine or juice, representing his blood.

Communion vessels: Vessels that hold communion elements of bread and wine—chalice and paten, respectively.

Confirmand: Person preparing to confirm baptismal vows.

Confirmation: Originally part of baptism, confirmation became a separate ritual (but not a sacrament) with the introduction of infant baptism; it is the time when persons confirm vows that were made for them at baptism; often preceded by study; someone who is baptized as a youth or adult has already confirmed their own baptism.

Easter: Sunday when we celebrate Jesus Christ's resurrection and victory over death and sin (Matthew 28:1-10, Mark 16:1-8, Luke 24:1-12, and John 20:1-23); date varies, according to lunar calendar. Worship may be held on Easter Day and Easter Eve (often called an Easter vigil). Preceded by the season of Lent, followed by the Great Fifty Days, ending in Pentecost.

Easter Vigil: Worship on Easter Eve (Saturday immediately before Easter), traditionally includes telling salvation history, lighting a paschal candle, and baptism. Date varies according to Easter.

Epiphany: January 6, celebration of Magi's visit (Wise Men, Matthew 2:1-12), revelation of Jesus to the world. Worship may be held on Epiphany or on Sunday preceding it. Preceded by Christmas and twelve days; followed by ordinary time.

Eucharist (see also Communion and Lord's Supper): Celebration of Christ's presence with us through bread and wine/juice, which represents his body and his blood; name recalls that meal is thanksgiving for all that God has done for us throughout the history of salvation.

Exegesis: Act of explaining and interpreting a biblical text, noting its context and appropriate application to the current day.

Font: Pool or place that holds water for sacrament of baptism.

Funeral pall (or, simply **pall**): Cloth that covers casket; reminds that through baptism we are clothed in Christ.

Great Fifty Days: Celebration of resurrection victory for fifty days, Easter to Pentecost, when risen Christ walked on earth, appearing to many and teaching (Acts 1:3); dates vary according to Easter and include Ascension.

Great Thanksgiving: Prayer of thanksgiving and blessing over communion elements of bread and cup.

Holy Week: Celebration of Palm Sunday through the last week of Jesus' life, including Holy Thursday and Good Friday. Dates vary according to Easter.

Invocation: Prayer that calls on the Holy Spirit's presence.

Laity: Every baptized Christian, distinguished in this word from *clergy*.

Lectern: Podium from which the Word is read, often where laity stand to lead worship.

Lent: Forty days (excluding Sundays) between Ash Wednesday and Easter in which we prepare for Easter and meditate on our baptismal vows.

Liturgical artists: Musicians, visual artists, dancers, actors, and other artists who are trained to work with liturgy, having artistic, theological, and liturgical training.

Liturgical colors: Used throughout history to visually signify seasons and holy days in the liturgical year. Currently in North America, the colors used are white (Christmas, Easter, baptism, marriage and funerals, purity and holiness), red (Holy Spirit, Pentecost, ordination), black (Good Friday/Jesus' crucifixion), purple (penitence, royalty of Jesus Christ, Lent and formerly for Advent), blue (now for Advent, hope and expectation), and green (ordinary time, spiritual growth).

Liturgical Renewal Movement: Started in the early 1900s and gained energy through **Vatican II**; has affected worship in many mainline and small denominations by focusing on active, holistic participation by all.

Liturgical season: Seasons (Advent, Lent, and so on) and holy days (Christmas, Easter, and so on) through the liturgical year.

Liturgical year: Calendar of the church; sometimes called *the church year*: Advent, Christmas, Epiphany, ordinary time, Ash Wednesday, Lent, Holy Week (Palm Sunday, Holy Thursday, Good Friday), Easter, the Great Fifty Days (including Ascension), Pentecost, and ordinary time (including World Communion Sunday and All Saints' Day).

Liturgy: From Greek, "the work of the people on behalf of the world." Denotes worship that is participatory and involves people using a variety of worship gifts.

Lord's Supper (see also Communion and Eucharist): Celebration of Christ's presence with us through bread and wine/juice, which represents his body and his blood; name recalls that the table belongs to Jesus, not to the church; not to be confused with the Last Supper, which occurred only once, during Jesus' physical time on earth.

Ordinary time: Refers to the use of ordinal numbers, 1st, 2nd, 3rd, etc. to denote Sundays after Pentecost (until The Reign of Christ Sunday and Advent) and Sundays after the Epiphany (until Transfiguration Sunday and Lent); seasons in the liturgical year that celebrate Jesus Christ's ministry, Holy Spirit's power, and God's continual work in our lives.

Palm/Passion Sunday: Sunday that begins Holy Week and celebrates triumphal entry of Jesus into Jerusalem (Matthew 21:1-11, Mark 11:1-11 and Luke 19:28-40) and his subsequent trials and death (Matthew 27:11-54, Mark 15:1-39, and Luke 23:1-49); time of celebration, challenge, and impending sorrow as society rejects Jesus over the coming week.

Paraments: Any cloth used on the altar table, on the lectern, in the pulpit, on the sanctuary walls, or within the worship space.

Paschal: From Hebrew, related to the Passover (Exodus 12–13) and God's liberation of us from slavery to sin and death; used as an adjective; in some languages is the basis for the word that is *Easter* in English.

Paschal candle: Large candle, used on Easter to represent the risen Christ; kept in chancel until Ascension when it is moved near the baptismal font; remainder of the year, lit at baptisms and at funerals (to recall baptism).

Paschal Mystery: Theological mystery surrounding Jesus Christ's work for our salvation—incarnation; ministries of teaching, healing, feeding; death, resurrection, ascension, and intercession for us. This mystery is always part of our worship celebration and is a particular focus during Lent through Pentecost.

Passion of Jesus Christ: His trials and death (Matthew 26:14–27:66, Mark 14:1–15:47, and Luke 22:14–23:56), linking him to the trials of humanity and to our salvation from sin and ultimately from death. *Passion* derives from words for *undergoing* or *martyrdom*, but in current usage, it also relates to the deep love/passion God showed for us through Jesus Christ.

Pastoral rites: In Protestant churches, rites that mark our life as holy and changed: confirmation, marriage, death, ordination, confession, and healing.

Paten: Plate that holds bread for communion.

Pentecost: Sunday fifty days after Easter that celebrates descent of the Holy Spirit and beginning of the church. Date varies with Easter.

Presider: Person who presides over sacraments of baptism and communion; also called a priest or pastor.

Public domain: Way of speaking about texts, including hymn texts and prayer texts, that denotes that they are no longer under copyright protection. In the United States, as of January 1, 2007, that includes everything published before 1923 that has not had its copyright renewed. More information at www.copyright.cornell.edu/training/Hirtle_Public_Domain.htm.

Pulpit: Podium from which the Word is proclaimed, that is, sermon is preached.

Reign of Christ Sunday: Last Sunday in ordinary time before the beginning of Advent; celebrates current and future reign of Jesus Christ.

Rite: Pattern of behavior, words and actions that mark a time, person, or place as holy.

Sacrament: "Outward sign of an invisible act"; shares root of *sacred*, "to make holy." Luther defined *sacrament* by three parts: means of grace, institution by Jesus Christ, and physical element (such as water, bread, or wine/juice). Protestant churches claim baptism and communion as sacraments.

Sacramental: Used increasingly to indicate that all of life is holy.

Sanctuary: Worship space in a church.

Saturday: Seventh day of week (Genesis 2:2-3); God rested from work of creation and blessed this day. Jewish tradition of understanding *day* as beginning with evening (Genesis 1:5b) makes Saturday evening an appropriate time for worship as it is the beginning of Sunday.

Sunday: First day of week (Genesis 1:1-5), when Jesus Christ was raised from death; each Sunday is celebration of light and resurrection (a "little Easter").

Transfiguration Sunday: Sunday before Ash Wednesday; celebrates Jesus' transfiguration (Matthew 17:1-9, Mark 9:2-9, and Luke 9:28-36).

Trinity: Christian understanding that God is revealed to humanity in three basic ways: through Creator and Father/Mother of us all, through Jesus Christ who came into human history as example and redeemer, and through the Holy Spirit, our sustainer and guide. Thus God is three-in-one and one-in-three, a model of community and diversity held inseparably together.

Trinity Sunday: Celebration of trinitarian nature of God, on the Sunday after Pentecost.

Vatican II: An Ecumenical Council of the Roman Catholic Church, 1962–1965; produced a document on worship called *Sacrosanctum Concilium* (*Constitution on the Sacred Liturgy*), calling for full, active, and conscious participation of everyone in worship. Along with the Liturgical Movement, this has affected Protestant worship as well as Roman Catholic.

Worship: "Attributing worth to" or *honoring,* this is the word most frequently used for gathering together to honor God and to remember who and whose we are.

Selected Bibliography

Bass, Diana Butler. *The Practicing Congregation: Imagining a New Old Church*. Herndon, Va.: The Alban Institute, 2004.

Callahan, Kennon L. *Small, Strong Congregations*. San Francisco: Jossey-Bass, 2000. See especially pages 152-87 on worship and music.

Doran, Carol, and Thomas H. Troeger. *Trouble at the Table: Gathering the Tribes for Worship*. Nashville: Abingdon Press, 1992.

Dudley, Carl S. *Effective Small Churches in the Twenty-first Century*. Nashville: Abingdon Press, 1978, 2003.

Kimball, Dan. *The Emerging Church*. Grand Rapids: Zondervan, 2003.

McLean, Terri Bocklund. *New Harmonies: Choosing Contemporary Music for Worship*. Bethesda, Md.: The Alban Institute, 1998.

Miller, Barbara Day. *The New Pastor's Guide to Leading Worship*. Nashville: Abingdon Press, 2006.

Ray, David R. *Wonderful Worship in Smaller Churches*. Cleveland: Pilgrim Press, 2000.

Redman, Robb. *The Great Worship Awakening: Singing a New Song in the Postmodern Church*. San Francisco: Jossey-Bass, 2002.

Rollins, Peter. *How (Not) to Speak of God*. Brewster, Mass.: Paraclete Press, 2006.

Songs and Prayers from Taizé (Community of Taizé). Chicago: GIA Publications, 1991.

Tisdale, Leonora Tubbs. *Preaching as Local Theology and Folk Art*. Minneapolis: Augsburg Fortress, 1997.

Wagley, Laurence A. *Preaching with the Small Congregation*. Nashville: Abingdon Press, 1989.

Ward, Pete. *Liquid Church*. Peabody, Mass.: Hendrickson, 2002.

Webber, Robert. *Planning Blended Worship: The Creative Mixture of Old and New*. Nashville: Abingdon Press, 1998.

White, James F. *Introduction to Christian Worship*. Nashville: Abingdon Press, 2001.

Helpful Organizations

Note: All websites and addresses are correct as of September 5, 2007.

The American Guild of English Handbell Ringers, www.agehr.org, 1055 E. Centerville Station Rd., Centerville, Ohio 45459.

The American Guild of Organists, www.agohq.org/home.html, 475 Riverside Drive, Suite 1260, New York, New York 10115.

The Association of Consultants for Liturgical Space, www.liturgical consultants.org.

The Association of Disciples Musicians, www.adm-doc.org/, Disciples Home Missions, P.O. Box 1986, Indianapolis, IN 46206.

Calvin Institute of Christian Worship, www.calvin.edu/worship/, 1855 Knollcrest Circle SE, Grand Rapids, MI 49546.

Choristers Guild (for children and youth singing and worship arts), www.choristersguild.org/, 2834 W. Kingsley Rd., Garland, TX 75041.

The Fellowship of United Methodists in Music and Worship Arts, www.fummwa.org/, P.O. Box 24787, Nashville, TN 37202.

The Hymn Society of The United States and Canada, www.the hymnsociety.org, 745 Commonwealth Ave., Boston, MA 02215.

Network of Biblical Storytellers, www.nobs.org/, Christian Theological Seminary, 1000 W. 42nd St., Indianapolis, IN 46208.

Presbyterian Association of Musicians, www.presbymusic.org/ index.htm, 100 Witherspoon Street, Louisville, KY 40202.

Sacred Dance Guild, www.sacreddanceguild.org, c/o Peggy Hoffman, P.O. Box 1046, Laurel, MD 20725.

Notes

Introduction

1. See Glossary for definitions of unfamiliar liturgical (worship) or church-related words.

2. Throughout this book I will use *congregation*, *worshiping group*, and *worshiping community* interchangeably; I do not mean to imply any sense of rigidity or traditionalism when I use the word *congregation*. The same is true about the terms *worship service* and *worship experience*.

3. *Kin-dom* is the form of *kingdom* used to suggest the vision of God's reign where human beings are all kin to one another and no one gender or race or culture dominates.

1. Worship

1. Phrasing from E. Bryon Anderson, "The Claims We Make About Worship" in *Proceedings of the North American Academy of Liturgy*, 2001, 91, and drawing on others.

2. John Wesley named worship as one of the means of grace, meaning that it is a channel for God's grace to flow into our lives and our world. Other means of grace are: prayer, searching the Scriptures, Holy Communion, fasting, and Christian conferencing (community). See his sermon "The Means of Grace."

3. Laurence H. Stookey, *Calendar: Christ's Time for the Church* (Nashville: Abingdon Press, 1996), 28-29.

4. Tex Sample, *Powerful Persuasion: Multimedia Witness in Christian Worship* (Nashville: Abingdon Press, 2005), 8-11.

5. L. Edward Phillips and Sara Webb Phillips, *In Spirit and Truth: United Methodist Worship for the Emerging Church; Equipping the Future Church* (Nashville: Discipleship Resources, 2000), 24.

6. David Ray, *Small Churches Are the Right Size* (New York: Pilgrim Press, 1982).

7. Dietrich Bonhoeffer, *Life Together* (London: SCM Press, 1954).

8. For a clear and challenging read on this, see Bill Easum, *Put on Your Own Oxygen Mask First: Rediscovering Ministry,* with Linnea Nilsen Capshaw (Nashville: Abingdon Press, 2004), 171-75.

2. Begin Where You Are

1. David Ray, *Small Churches Are the Right Size* (New York: Pilgrim Press, 1982), 57.

2. Lyle Schaller, *Small Congregation, Big Potential: Ministry in the Small Membership Church* (Nashville: Abingdon Press, 2003), 167.

3. Christine D. Pohl, *Making Room: Recovering Hospitality As a Christian Tradition* (Grand Rapids: Eerdmans, 1999), 67, based on Matthew 25:31-46.

4. From information available in a good study Bible, such as *The New Interpreter's Study Bible*, Abingdon Press, 2003.

5. Many denominational worship books or commentaries include information on the use of art in worship. See also the list of organizations at the end of this book that can be helpful in learning to use the arts in worship, and Janet R. Walton, *Art and Worship: A Vital Connection* (Collegeville, Minn.: Liturgical Press, 1988, 1991).

6. For a detailed study see Millard B. Knowles, "The Reshaping of Biblical Preaching Through Recovery of the Oral Traditions of Biblical Storytelling" (PhD Diss., United Theological Seminary, 1993).

3. Our Context

1. Gordon Lathrop, *Central Things: Worship in Word and Sacrament* (Minneapolis: Augsburg Fortress, 2005), 13-14.

2. James F. White and Susan F. White, *Church Architecture: Building and Renovating for Christian Worship* (Nashville: Abingdon Press, 1988; repr., Akron, Ohio: OSL Publications, 1998).

3. See chapter 5 for words around the reading of Scripture that also honor it.

4. See chapter 6 for scriptures related to baptism that would be appropriate for banners.

5. White and White, *Church Architecture,* 15-16.

6. See chapter 7, "Creating or Commissioning Art for Your Worship."

7. See chapter 5, "Hearing the Word."

8. See chapter 6 for more ideas.

9. See chapter 6 for other ideas on distributing/receiving communion.

10. For an engaging narrative of an early worship experience in a house, see *Going to Church in the First Century* by Robert Banks (Jacksonville, Fla.: Seedsowers, 1990).

11. See below for specifics on outdoor space as it has its own opportunities and challenges.

12. See chapter 6 for more ideas.

13. See below for more on river or lake baptisms.

14. See chapter 6 for more ideas.

15. Although some suggest that drowning is part of the point of baptism, having candidates so fearful that they cannot experience God's grace is counterproductive.

16. That is, we have made so much of the notion that God is Three, without equally reminding ourselves that God is One, that we venture into tritheism, worshiping three gods rather than one.

4. Getting Ready to Plan the Weekly Service

1. Readings for the lectionary may be found in many worship books, hymnals, and online at www.textweek.com.

2. Ruth Duck, *Finding Words for Worship* (Louisville: Westminster John Knox, 1995).

3. One good resource that names and defines these sorts of terms throughout the lectionary readings is Carolyn Brown's excellent volumes of resources for children and worship, *Forbid Them Not* (3 vols. [one for each lectionary year]; Nashville: Abingdon Press, 1991–1993).

4. Tim Ladwig, *Psalm 23* (Grand Rapids: Eerdmans, 1997).

5. Planning the Actual Service

1. Brad Berglund, *Reinventing Sunday: Breakthrough Ideas for Transforming Worship* (Valley Forge, Pa.: Judson Press, 2001).

2. Two online sources that many persons find useful are http://bible.oremus.org and www.biblegateway.com.

3. For examples, see *Palm Sunday and Holy Week Services*, by Robin Knowles Wallace (Nashville: Abingdon Press, 2006).

4. Laurence Wagley, *Preaching with the Small Congregation* (Nashville: Abingdon Press, 1989). Also Ernesto Cardenal and Donald D. Walsh, *The Gospel in Solentiname* (4 vols.; Maryknoll, N.Y.: Orbis Books, 1982), another example of congregations engaging in interpreting the scriptures for their lives.

5. In his important work on the theology and practice of worship, *Holy People: A Liturgical Ecclesiology* (Minneapolis: Fortress Press, 1999), Gordon Lathrop relies heavily on the principle of juxtaposition to describe how each element of worship and our understanding of it is enlivened and challenged by juxtaposition.

6. www.habitat.org/, Partner Service Center, 121 Habitat St., Americus, GA 31709.

7. www.bread.org/, 50 F Street, NW, Suite 500, Washington, DC 20001.

8. www.heifer.org, 1 World Avenue, Little Rock, AR 72202.

9. Amnesty International (www.amnesty.org), 5 Penn Plaza, 14th floor, New York, NY 10001; local prison Bible study group; or Kairos Prison Ministry International (www.kairosprisonministry.org), 130 University Park Dr., Suite 170, Winter Park, FL 32792.

10. See chapter 7 for more about laying on of hands.

11. Phrase from Carlton R. Young, *Music of the Heart: John and Charles Wesley on Music and Musicians* (Carol Stream, Ill.: Hope Publishing, 1995).

6. Baptism and Communion

1. Some denominations include foot washing among the sacraments or ordinances. Luther himself wondered early on if penance and the forgiveness that it brings might be a sacrament, but the physical element was unclear. Some denominations are unclear about the status of confirmation, although study of the early church and baptism makes it clear that confirmation is a renewal or seal of baptism.

2. For this and additional ideas and prayers for communion, see *Communion Services* by Robin Knowles Wallace (Nashville: Abingdon Press, 2006).

3. A video that demonstrates these options and reflects active congregational participation in communion is *Lift Up Your Hearts: The Eucharistic Prayer* (23 minutes; Chicago: Liturgy Training Publications, 1994). Although this is filmed in a Roman Catholic congregation, many ideas and practices are adaptable for Protestants.

4. Knowles Wallace, *Communion Services*, 11-12.

7. The Arts in Worship

1. Carlton R. Young, *Music of the Heart: John and Charles Wesley on Music and Musicians* (Carol Stream, Ill.: Hope Publishing, 1995).

2. John L. Bell, *The Singing Thing: A Case for Congregational Song* (Chicago: GIA Publications, 2000).

8. Select Ideas for Congregations up to One Hundred

1. See pages 55-57 on adapting resources.

2. Many Christian bookstores now sell oils or balms for anointing; you can also create your own by combining olive oil with a drop of aromatic oil (keep the fragrance weak in case of allergies).